HIGH ROAD LEADERSHIP

HIGH ROAD LEADERSHIP

BRINGING PEOPLE TOGETHER
IN A WORLD THAT DIVIDES

High Road Leadership: Bringing People Together in a World That Divides

Copyright © 2024 by John C. Maxwell

All rights reserved. No part of this publication may be reproduced, stored in a retrieval system, or transmitted in any form by any means, electronic, mechanical, photocopy, recording, or otherwise, without the prior permission of the publisher, except as provided by USA copyright law.

No patent liability is assumed with respect to the use of the information contained herein. Although every precaution has been taken in the preparation of this book, the publisher and author assume no responsibility for errors or omissions. Neither is any liability assumed for damages resulting from the use of the information contained herein.

Scripture quotations marked NIV are taken from the Holy Bible, New International Version®, NIV®. Copyright © 1973, 1978, 1984, 2011 by Biblica, Inc.® Used by permission of Zondervan. All rights reserved worldwide. www.zondervan.com. The "NIV" and "New International Version" are trademarks registered in the United States Patent and Trademark Office by Biblica, Inc.®

Scripture quotations marked MSG are taken from THE MESSAGE. Copyright © 1993, 2002, 2018 by Eugene H. Peterson. Used by permission of NavPress. All rights reserved. Represented by Tyndale House Publishers, a Division of Tyndale House Ministries.

Published by Maxwell Leadership Publishing, an imprint of Forefront Books, Nashville, Tennessee.

Distributed by Simon & Schuster.
Library of Congress Control Number: 2024902981

Print ISBN: 978-1-6376-3441-7
E-book ISBN: 979-8-8871-0035-7

Cover Design by Bruce Gore, Gore Studio, Inc.
Interior Design by Bill Kersey, KerseyGraphics

Printed in India by Replika Press Pvt. Ltd.

10 9 8 7 6 5 4 3 2 1

*This book is dedicated to Mo Anderson.
Farmgirl, teacher, CEO, Oklahoma Hall-of-Fame member,
and real estate legend, you have been a beacon of light in the
world of business. Every decision you make is filtered through
your high standards. Every person you lead is treated with
dignity and respect. Every victory you achieve is always
a win-win. Your standards are high ... and your integrity
is even higher. You have always brought people together
in a world that divides. I am glad to call you friend.*

CONTENTS

ACKNOWLEDGMENTS 9

1. BRING PEOPLE TOGETHER 11
2. VALUE ALL PEOPLE 31
3. ACKNOWLEDGE YOUR HUMANNESS 47
4. DO THE RIGHT THINGS FOR THE RIGHT REASONS 65
5. GIVE MORE THAN YOU TAKE 83
6. DEVELOP EMOTIONAL CAPACITY 99
7. PLACE PEOPLE ABOVE YOUR OWN AGENDA 121
8. EMBRACE AUTHENTICITY 137
9. TAKE ACCOUNTABILITY FOR YOUR ACTIONS 155
10. LIVE BY THE BIGGER PICTURE 171
11. DON'T KEEP SCORE 189
12. DESIRE THE BEST FOR OTHERS 205

NOTES 221

ABOUT THE AUTHOR 233

ACKNOWLEDGMENTS

I want to say thank you to Charlie Wetzel and the rest of the team who assisted me with thinking through and writing this book: Jared Cagle, Mark Cole, Linda Eggers, Erin Miller, and Stephanie Wetzel. I also thank the people in my organizations who support me. You all add incredible value to me, which allows me to add value to others. Together, we're making a difference!

1
BRING PEOPLE TOGETHER

For more than fifty years, I have committed my life to helping people lead better. At the age of twenty-five, I came to the conclusion that everything rises and falls on leadership. That realization motivated me to give my life to studying and teaching leadership. In fact, today I am even more convinced of the crucial importance of leadership than at any other time in my life. But the state of leadership today makes me incredibly sad as a leader.

Leadership can be a blessing or a curse. It can help people rise to a better life, or it can cause people to fall into despair. I have personally witnessed both outcomes. My organizations are dedicated to achieving the former goal. Maxwell Leadership has trained and certified fifty thousand coaches in seventy-two countries. In the past, my nonprofit organizations trained more than five million leaders around the world, and today they are working with leaders in six nations to promote transformation in their countries. Whether I'm interacting with business leaders, volunteers, or government leaders, when I've finished working with them, I ask them these questions: How are your people? Are they better or worse off as a result of your leadership? In other words, are the people rising or falling because *you* are their leader?

What's sad is that we are living in a world where disagreement reigns and, instead of conditions getting better for people because of good leadership, people are becoming disillusioned and bitter because of bad leadership. In the United States, many people pick a side and turn against everybody they see as being on *the other side*. In our culture, there is a chasm between *us* and *them*. On our side are the people who think, act, look, vote, eat, live, speak, and work like us. On the other side is everyone else. People spend their time fighting about many issues we shouldn't be fighting over. Even when someone "wins," it's a bad win because it's not a win for most people.

WHY ARE THINGS GOING DOWNHILL?

What makes the difference between good and bad leaders? What causes the rise or fall of the leadership that impacts people? Skills and values. Leadership *rises* when leaders possess good leadership skills and good values. It *falls* when leaders' skills or values are poor. It may be obvious that leaders who lack good skills are incapable of helping people. What's less obvious is the impact on people when leaders don't possess good values. If the values and skills are both lacking, leaders drag the people down with them. If their skills are good and their values are bad, they manipulate people for their own benefit. As a leader, whenever you move people for your own advantage, it creates a win-lose situation, which is always wrong.

Good Skills & Good Values	Leaders Raise Up Their People
Poor Skills & Good Values	Leaders Can't Help Their People
Good Skills & Poor Values	Leaders Manipulate Their People
Poor Skills & Poor Values	Leaders Drag Down Their People

So now you know why I'm sad as a leader. Today I see more falling than rising in the leadership world. My sadness has moved me to write this book.

LOOKING FOR WAYS TO DIVIDE

Unfortunately, in the United States politics sets the standard for how people treat each other, and it isn't positive. You can easily see the shift in leaders at the top in presidential elections. In the past, candidates would fight hard against one another, but after the election, they would acknowledge each other's efforts, shake hands, and say, "Good match." Then they'd work with everyone from both sides until the next election. It was like a boxing match or mixed martial arts bout where two fighters beat each other up but showed good sportsmanship at the end by shaking hands. They respect the other person's commitment and sacrifice, and as a result, they experience a sense of brotherhood or sisterhood because they're both fighters and know what it takes to enter the ring. That can create a natural bond.

> Leadership rises when leaders possess good leadership skills and good values.

Today, politics is less like sport and more like war. Politicians fight hard, and they have little respect for their opponents. Some appear to genuinely hate each other. At the end of the race, their attitude seems to be, "I fought hard. I won. You don't deserve to get a say. Your side needs to submit to me!" No wonder a recent poll found that 63 percent of Americans have little confidence in elected officials, 67 percent have "not too much" or "no confidence" in the federal government, and 70 percent believe lower trust in people makes it harder to solve the country's problems.[1] Unfortunately, at the same time, people look at politics and think, *This is how we should do things*, and they follow their lead. What a mess! We can't build anything worthwhile on hate. As Maya Angelou said, "Hate, it has caused a lot of problems in the world but has not solved one yet."[2]

DISRESPECT HAS BECOME COMMON

This propensity to fight and disrespect other people has spread and bled into nearly every aspect of life. It is becoming increasingly difficult for us to work with one another and to accomplish worthy goals. Illinois governor JB Pritzker pointed out the negative way people treat one another in a commencement address he delivered to the 2023 graduates at Northwestern University. To entertain his audience, he used quotes from the American television show *The Office*. One quote by the fictional character Dwight Schrute gained a lot of attention: "Whenever I'm about to do something, I think, *Would an idiot do that?* And if they would, I do not do that thing." Pritzker went on to explain how the "worst kinds of idiots" are people who are cruel to others:

> "Hate, it has caused a lot of problems in the world but has not solved one yet."
> – Maya Angelou

> Somewhere along the way in the last few years, our society has come to believe that weaponized cruelty is part of some well-thought-out master plan. Cruelty is seen by some as an adroit cudgel to gain power. Empathy and kindness are considered weak. Many important people look at the vulnerable only as rungs on a ladder to the top. I'm here to tell you that when someone's path through this world is marked with acts of cruelty, they have failed the first test of an advanced society. They never forced their animal brain to evolve past its first instinct. They never forged new mental pathways to overcome their own instinctual fears, and so their thinking and problem solving will lack the imagination and creativity that the kindest people have in spades.

Over my many years in politics and business I have found one thing to be universally true: the kindest person in the room is often the smartest.[3]

Kindness, consideration, and empathy used to comprise the minimum standard of conduct when we interacted with one another, but too many people no longer embrace and practice those values. According to Gallup, 50 percent of Americans rate the overall state of moral values in the US as poor. And more than 75 percent of Americans believe morals are getting worse. They cite the greatest problem as a lack of consideration for others.[4] And based on my experience traveling around the world, I'd guess the statistics in other countries would be the same or, in some cases, even worse.

> **More than 75 percent of Americans believe morals are getting worse. They cite the greatest problem as a lack of consideration for others.**

People have always disagreed with one another. Talk to any other person in the world, and you can find *something* you disagree about. Why should we let that bother us? Margaret and I love each other dearly and have been married for more than fifty years, yet we don't agree on everything. My CEO, Mark Cole, and I don't agree on everything, yet we've worked well together every day for more than twenty years. What we've accomplished together is significant. Nobody agrees on everything, and nobody is right all the time.

DISAGREEMENT? OFTEN. DISRESPECT? NEVER!

One of the reasons we don't come together and work with one another is that we no longer see people on the other side as merely disagreeing. We see them as disagreeable human beings. We assume their motives are wrong. And the moment we think a person's motives are wrong, we lose trust.

There's a significant difference between believing the other side's *ideas* are wrong and believing their *motives* are wrong. If I think people are wrong in their opinions or ideas, I'll be willing to engage in discussion and seek common ground. However, if I think their motivation is wrong, I'll draw lines, build walls, and refuse to engage in any kind of positive conversation because I believe they mean to do harm. That ends the relationship.

> No matter what the circumstances, if we want to be good leaders, we must come to the table, sit in the middle without choosing a side, listen to others, and work to bring people together.

Most of us today seem to possess a very strong confirmation bias. We seek out information and data that confirm what we already believe, ignoring all the rest. We listen to experts whose opinions confirm our own. We don't want to entertain or weigh opposing views. We want *our* views affirmed.

Good leaders need to rise above this attitude and help the people they lead do the same. How? We need to possess a strong *collaboration* bias. We need to bring people together to increase our understanding of each other and broaden our perspective.

Good leaders bear the weight of responsibility for finding the best answers for any challenge or problem. They understand that neither they, their team, nor their "side" may know the best solutions. As a result, they commit themselves to remaining open-minded and listening to everyone, including people who oppose them or who are on the other side. This is true in any kind of setting. Bill Haslam, a success in business as well as government, where he served two terms as the mayor of Knoxville and two terms as governor of Tennessee, believes that task is easier in business organizations than in the public sector. He observed, "In a well-run company, the workforce, leadership, and board are all unified in the purpose and mission of the business. That's not true in a government. In government, there are almost as many visions for what the government should do and be as there are citizens. Often, leadership in government means balancing competing valid interests."[5] No matter what the circumstances, if we want to be good leaders, we must come to the table, sit in the middle without choosing a side, listen to others, and work to bring people together.

WE NEED EACH OTHER

If you're a leader and you allow yourself to get drawn into taking sides and working against other groups of people, you're limiting your leadership. As leaders, we all *need* the people on the other side. Our side doesn't have all the answers. Believing we do is arrogant. I'm not always right, and neither are you. And those on the "other side" are not always wrong. If you don't listen to them, you're shrinking your influence and limiting your impact. If you can't work with people who disagree with you, you will never become the leader you could be. No one will ever convince me that you can choose only half of the people and get as much done as if you work to lead *all* the people.

> **If you can't work with people who disagree with you, you will never become the leader you could be.**

You lose the *best* way when you must always have your *own* way. If you become entrenched on one side and spend your time fighting for it, everyone eventually loses. This path of mistrust and division will never lead us anywhere we want to go. We can't divide people and expect to accomplish positive results. Conversation and collaboration will always come up with better answers than isolation and exclusion.

Let's face it. It's easier to find agreement with people like you, who are against the same things you're against. Politics today is built on rallying people around what they're against. Candidates are trained to build their stump speeches on what's wrong because it incites a stronger emotional response in voters. From there, the politician hopes to engage in a transaction: "Vote for me, and I'll do something about this thing we hate." But when leaders take sides, build their lives on what they're against, and win at the expense of others, it creates an environment and culture of haves and have-nots. The winners get the spoils, the losers get the shaft, and the people in power do whatever they can to get their way and stay in power. This is what many white people in the United States did during slavery, Reconstruction, and the Jim Crow era. This is what many leaders do today in developing countries and nations with authoritarian regimes. Whoever is in power characterizes their side as right, and the other side as wrong and inferior.

As we look at the current state of leadership, if we think all these problems have been created by "the other side," we're missing the point. If we want a better culture, a better country, and a better world, we need to look in the mirror and recognize our own contributions to the division we're experiencing. We need to have a change of heart and mind in how we treat people. Instead of widening the chasm between us, we need to build bridges and move toward others while looking for common ground. The way to do that is to become a leader who takes the high road. That is what this book is about.

THE THREE ROADS WE CAN TAKE

I believe people choose one of three paths when they interact with others: the low road, the middle road, or the high road. As I describe them, you'll recognize people you know based on how they treat others. Let's start with the middle road because that's where most people tend to travel.

The Middle Road

When we travel the middle road, we value fairness. We are open to give-and-take to keep things even. We think, *I have received this much, so I should give that much*. We are willing to compromise—as long as we're getting at least as much as we're giving, and we'd prefer that we get our share first.

That can work if we are trying to be positive, though this kind of mindset is limiting because it is very transactional. What about on the negative side? When people taking the middle road get hurt or taken advantage of, their natural reaction is to take an equal measure of revenge. Old Testament law states, "But if there is serious injury, you are to take life for life, eye for eye, tooth for tooth, hand for hand, foot for foot, burn for burn, wound for wound, bruise for bruise."[6] But that doesn't bring people together. As Mahatma Gandhi is reputed to have said, "An eye for an eye makes the whole world blind."[7]

> "An eye for an eye makes the whole world blind." – Attributed to Mahatma Gandhi

I understand why many people choose the middle road. It makes sense. It seems to promise security. We can calculate what we give and what we get to try to keep everything in balance. We can seek justice when we've been wronged. When democratic governments work, their leaders often take the middle road, with people coming to the table willing to compromise. They will give something in order to get something.

But there are downsides to middle-road thinking. We *might* be willing to work with people on the other side, but we want the other side to make the first move. We want *them* to listen first, then maybe we will decide to listen too. We want *them* to acknowledge the good ideas our side offers first, and then maybe we will be open to their ideas. We want *them* to be fair first, to change, to give us justice, and to make things right. Then—maybe—we will treat them the same way. Until then, we wait. And sadly, we often continue to wait.

Another downside of the middle road is that if we take it, we will always be calculating and keeping score. What many don't know is that they're missing a whole level of living that can't be achieved through calculation. They're missing out on the greater blessing that comes from living and giving on the high road.

The Low Road

Before we examine the high road, let's look at the low. Where people on the middle road strive for fairness, people on the low road think only of themselves. On the low road, they look out for number one, as the old saying goes. Truly, we're all naturally selfish. I know I am. But low-road leaders take from others and don't even think about giving anything back. Why? Because they believe taking is the only way they can get what they want. If they don't do whatever it takes to get what they desire, they believe they will be left out or get left behind.

I've also observed that more and more people who travel the low road think the world *owes* them. They see themselves as victims. So when they take from others, they believe they are settling a score or making the world fair for themselves. But because they consistently take from others to get what they want, they are actually making the world *less fair*. They are taking advantage of others for the benefit of themselves or their side. And when low-road people have positions of leadership, they do even greater damage because they devalue other people. They belittle, criticize, and undermine others to get what they want or maintain the upper hand.

Leaders on the low road leverage the chasm that separates people. If they could, they would *widen* it. If they can't, they'll settle for talking about how deep and wide and uncrossable it is. They don't *want* to build bridges. They keep people divided as much as they can because they believe it will help them maintain whatever position and power they have.

Low-road people can suck the life out of others because they think only of themselves and getting what they want. Ironically, even though they are constantly taking, they are never satisfied. They live in a perpetual state of neediness. The more they take, the more they want. The cycle never ends.

The High Road

Where the middle and low roads are me-first, the high road is others first. High-road people intentionally give first without worrying about receiving anything back. They aren't trying to make their interactions fair, because they acknowledge life isn't fair. They value every person and treat each one well whether that individual is traveling on the low, middle, or high road. As a result, they want to keep the balance in the *other* person's favor because they know it makes the world a better place. And they don't worry about not getting their share because they believe there's enough to go around for everyone.

> Being a high-road leader doesn't make you *better* than others.

The Cambridge dictionary says the meaning of "take the high road" is "to behave in a moral way when other people are not behaving morally."[8] But when I refer to the high road, that's not exactly what I'm advocating. High-road leadership has nothing to do with being morally superior or righteous. The high road is not necessarily the moral high ground. Being a high-road leader doesn't make you *better* than others. Nor is traveling the high road simply a matter of good character. Yes, high-road people have good character, but so do many middle-road people.

The ability to take the high road requires something more. It requires the right mindset. Instead of focusing on self, we must focus on the well-being of others. Instead of promoting ourselves, we must promote others. Instead of gathering attention for our benefit, we must direct it to others. We must look for the good in people to try to bring out their best. This is a mindset anyone can choose to adopt. And when we find ourselves engaging in low-road behavior, which everyone does at times, we shouldn't make excuses. We should correct ourselves, make amends, and return to the high road.

Now that you understand the three roads, compare them side by side:

High-Road Leaders	Middle-Road Leaders	Low-Road Leaders
Value Others	Seek Value from Others	Devalue Others
Bring People Together	Move Back and Forth	Divide People
Close the Gap between People	Live with the Gap between People	Widen the Gap between People
Give More Than They Receive	Give Equal to What They've Received	Take More Than They Give
Give First	Give Back	Give Nothing
Don't Keep Score (Unconditional Giving)	Keep Score (Conditional Giving)	Don't Keep Score (Unconditional Taking)
Want *You* to Win	Want *Us* to Win	Want *Me* to Win
Treat Others Better Than They Are Treated	Treat Others the Same as They Are Treated	Treat Themselves at Others' Expense

If you want to help create a better world, commit to being a high-road leader. Treating others better than they treat you, and with consistency and without judgmentalism, is the best way to bring people together, and it's the only way to make the changes we want to see in our world.

LESSONS FROM MOM AND DAD

I've tried to live and lead on the high road, but I think a lot of the credit for that belongs to my parents. I won the parent lottery. I knew I was unconditionally loved by my mother. She pointed out my flaws and corrected me while still loving me completely. That helped me know myself and accept myself as I was. The great sense of security that resulted caused me not to think the worst about others. Receiving unconditional love made me want to give it to others.

If you received unconditional love, you've got a good foundation for valuing others and taking the high road with people. But even if you didn't, please know that you can still choose that pathway. While everyone else is judging people, you

> Treating others better than they treat you, and with consistency and without judgmentalism, is the best way to bring people together.

can extend them grace. When everyone else is taking from them, you can give. Think about the positive impact you could make by doing that. If you're not sure whether it's worth the effort, just think about how you would feel if somebody forgave you, encouraged you, showed you grace when you fell short.

My mother taught me to *see* people the right way. My father taught me to *treat* people the right way. What they gave me, I want to share with you.

WHY THE HIGH ROAD IS THE BEST ROAD

I know of no better way to live and lead than on the high road. The high road is not only a better way of living and the best way of leading others; it also yields many practical benefits that produce better results:

1. The High Road Brings People Together

High-road leaders don't focus on the chasm between people. They focus on connection. They build bridges instead of walls. They find common ground to build bridges so they can get to where other people are. They intentionally take steps of faith toward other people. They are willing to go first, give first, serve first, trust first. They know these are the steps toward creating better relationships, workplaces, neighborhoods, communities, cities, countries, and cultures.

2. The High Road Brings Out the Best in People

High-road leadership is about valuing people according to their potential. I've always found that when you believe the best about people and give them your best, it brings out *their* best. When you value people and add value to them, you create a world of value. If you want to be a high-road leader, you must always try to give more than you receive. You will have to treat people well on their bad days as well as their good ones. Is it true that if you always take the high road some people will take advantage of you? Yes. But that's their problem. High-road leaders don't get angry or try to get even. They just move on and work with others who desire to become their best.

> High-road leaders don't focus on the chasm between people. They focus on connection.

3. The High Road Creates Winners Without Creating Losers

More and more leaders today see leadership as a zero-sum game, where the only way to win is to make sure the other person loses.

When you take the high road, you don't try to create losers, and you don't see every disagreement as a war. If you define a win as *giving first*, how can you lose? You can take pleasure in helping others better themselves and their situation. You can make sure the other person wins first. And if you receive something in return, it creates a win-win. That's a bonus.

4. The High Road Has Less Traffic

If you become a high-road leader, you will be taking the road less traveled. While you are serving others and bringing people together, other

> When you believe the best about people and give them your best, it brings out *their* best.

leaders will be serving themselves. Most will be traveling the middle way. The worst will be on the low road. If you take the high road, you will stand out because your actions will be so different from others'. That will get you noticed as a leader. It will attract others to you because most people enjoy spending time with leaders who are positive and generous. And by traveling on the high road, you will experience a better life because it truly is more blessed to give than receive.

5. The High Road Is the Path to Significance

When your focus is on only yourself and what you can achieve, you may become *successful*. This is the path many people travel in life. But *significance* lies on the path of helping others and making the world better. If you will work to see things from other people's perspectives, make the shift toward adding value to them, and start helping them regardless of whether it benefits you, your life will become more fulfilling. You will experience significance, which is far more lasting than success.

MY CLIMB TO A HIGHER ROAD

My parents set a great example for me, but I must admit, I didn't start out as a high-road leader. Like many people, I began as a middle-road leader who wanted to get his needs met first. When I started leading in my first position, I was constantly recruiting people and trying to persuade them to buy into my vision. I believed that if they would help me, they would benefit from being part of something greater than themselves, and I also wanted to add value to them along the way. But then one day I went to see Zig Ziglar speak at a convention, and he said something that grabbed my attention: "You can have everything in life you want, if you will just help enough other people get what they want."

> Significance lies on the path of helping others and making the world better.

That was a revelation to me. I realized I needed to reach out to people, find out what they needed, and help them get it. *Then* I would get what I need. This was an important step toward the high road. It didn't put me *on* the high road. I was still on the middle road, and my thinking was still transactional, but it prompted me to start giving first. And that's when I began to discover the fulfillment that comes from helping others. I got a taste of significance, and I became convinced that human beings were created for significance, not mere success.

I believe if you make the first move by placing others ahead of yourself and adding value to them, you will begin to feel fulfilled. That will make you worry less about whether it benefits you directly. Too many people miss out on this because they don't realize they must take this first step. But once you experience the joy of helping others, you'll never want to turn back. And eventually, if you keep going to others first and giving first, you can become a high-road leader.

THE PRACTICES OF HIGH-ROAD LEADERS

I've given a lot of thought to what it means to be a high-road leader, and I've talked about it with many people. What I believe is that all high-road leaders share common practices. If you are to be a high-road leader, you must do these twelve things:

- Bring People Together
- Value All People
- Acknowledge Your Humanness
- Do the Right Things for the Right Reasons
- Give More Than You Take
- Develop Emotional Capacity
- Place People Above Your Own Agenda
- Embrace Authenticity
- Be Accountable for Your Actions
- Live by the Bigger Picture
- Don't Keep Score
- Desire the Best for Others

Every time you take these actions, you are traveling the high road in leadership. You are leading to serve others, not just yourself.

I must warn you: High-road leadership requires patience. Bringing people together takes time. But striving to stay on the high road is worth the effort. Yes, there are times you will make low-road decisions or engage in low-road behaviors. All of us do. When those things happen, don't pull away from others in embarrassment. When you sense you've done something wrong, admit your fault, apologize, and make things right if you can. That puts you back on the right path to the high road. And here's some great news: when we make U-turns like that, we can travel light in this world. We won't hold grudges, we'll rebound faster after mistakes, and we won't be weighed down by guilt or hobbled by second-guessing. What leader doesn't want that?

FOLLOW THE (HIGH-ROAD) LEADER

If you've never witnessed people practicing high-road leadership, you may have a difficult time believing it's possible and trusting the process. And this is a problem. Many young people today have never seen good models of high-road leadership. Most of the leadership examples they've seen come from politics, entertainment, or social media. If that's where you've received your modeling, then you've seen more than your share of the low road. But that doesn't mean you have to go in that direction. You can enjoy living another way.

Seek out living examples of high-road leadership. If you can't find any, learn by reading about high-road leaders past and present. One that I admire most is Abraham Lincoln. We think people today live in a divided time! He faced much worse division and racial conflict. While the different sides today fight with words, in his time they fought with guns and bayonets. Nobody looks at Abraham Lincoln and says he had no problems to deal with.

In the face of all that, he continually took the high road with others. He didn't try to win public opinion. He didn't defend himself when he was insulted. He took the blame when his generals failed. He left his office door open—literally—so that anyone could walk in off the street and talk to him. He even filled his presidential cabinet with his opponents because he was aware that he didn't have all the answers, and having his ideas challenged made him better. He never believed that people who had different perspectives or opinions were wrong or evil, the way people do today. He was humble and open enough to listen to his opponents, learn from them, change, give them credit, and help the country.

Wouldn't it be wonderful if leaders didn't serve themselves today? How can we change that? By changing ourselves first. By choosing to take the high road and encouraging others to do the same. If you have that desire, then turn the page and read on. Each of the following chapters teaches a leadership practice that will help you live on the high road. There's no telling what you might be able to accomplish if you travel that road. But even if you don't do all that you hope, you will live with fewer regrets. And the people you touch along the way will benefit greatly.

The Pathway to Bringing People Together:
COMMON GROUND

The fastest and most proven way to bring people together in a world that divides is to find common ground. I've touched on this throughout this chapter. When you find common ground, you create ways forward that didn't exist before. When you bring people together you make it possible for them to work together to improve their team, organization, neighborhood, city, and culture.

To be a high-road leader, when your instincts tell you to fight, you need to extend a hand of friendship. When others build walls, you need to look for a gate. When others say you have nothing in common, you need to double your efforts to discover something—anything—you share in common so that you can create a way to meet and build a relationship. High-road leaders are connectors.

2
VALUE ALL PEOPLE

HAVE YOU EVER HAD A CONVERSATION THAT WAS NO BIG DEAL TO the person who gave you advice, but it changed the trajectory of your life? I engaged in one of those the day I graduated from college. It occurred at dinner that night. I was sitting at the table with my parents; my fiancée, Margaret; and my siblings, Larry and Trish. I was on the cusp of transitioning into my adult professional life. In a few days, Margaret and I would get married and go on our honeymoon. As soon as we got back, we would move to Hillham, Indiana, where I had accepted my first position as the pastor of a small country church. As we sat and ate, I asked my dad a simple question: "What's the best advice you can give me as I start my career?"

> "Value people, believe in them, and love them unconditionally. Do those things every day, and you will be successful." – *Melvin Maxwell*

Dad was a pastor who'd led successful, growing churches. He'd also served as a district leader of pastors, and he was currently leading the college I'd just graduated from as its president, so he had a wealth of experience and wisdom.

"Son," Dad replied, "value people, believe in them, and love them unconditionally. Do those things every day, and you will be successful."

I don't recall whether we talked more about it, and I don't think the conversation was long. That may have been all he said. What I remember is that his words resonated deep within me. I had seen my father value everyone he met. I had seen him express his belief in people thousands of times. And I had seen him be kind and loving to all sorts of people. On top of that, I'd experienced the unconditional love that my mother gave. So I understood his advice, and it made sense. I told myself, *I'm going to do that.*

STARTING OUT ON THE RIGHT FOOT

Valuing people, believing in them, and loving them unconditionally became the framework for everything I did as I started my career. When I met people for the first time, I showed them that I valued them. As I worked with people in the church, I expressed my belief in them. I reached out to as many people as I could in the community. Even when I was leading meetings with the board or planning events, I worked to demonstrate those values. I was a young, inexperienced leader with the desire to produce and achieve. I believe embracing these values helped me to take a kinder and a gentler approach to leading others than I might have otherwise. And people responded very positively.

I even brought those values into my speaking. Every time I communicated, my desire was to express how much I valued the people in my audience, how I believed in them, and how much I loved them. I wanted to empower people, build them up, and inspire them to grow and change. To do that, I always tried to communicate in positive terms. How can anyone demonstrate a positive belief in people by being negative? It just doesn't work. I emphasized what people *could do*, not what they *should not do*. That set me apart from many of my colleagues in other churches.

That's not to say I was doing everything right. While I was getting a lot done in my church and being recognized in my career, I was also driven by my own selfish desire to be liked. I was a people pleaser. When someone didn't like me, I would do whatever was needed to win them over. Because I'm naturally good with people, I could usually figure out how to accomplish that. But I had to learn that it was more important for me to love people than for them to love me if I was to become a more effective leader. You can't effectively *lead* people if you *need* people.

In hindsight, I recognize that I was learning to practice high-road leadership, though I wouldn't have called it that back then. I was simply following my dad's advice and my own instincts. These values became the core of my leadership. And Dad's advice was right. Treating people the way he suggested did make me successful; adding additional leadership skills made it possible for me to cast vision, equip people, and take an organization where it needed to go. By the time I was twenty-five years old, I was leading the most respected church in the denomination. At age twenty-eight, I was the most influential person in the denomination. And the success I experienced gave me the confidence to believe I could have a greater impact in the wider world.

HOW TO VALUE ALL PEOPLE

If you want to become the best leader you can be, you need to learn how to lead people on the high road. How can you do that? Start by valuing all people. Here's what that means:

Embrace the Value of *All* People

At the heart of high-road leadership is willingness to value all people. That is the start of everything. If you don't accept and embrace the idea that all people have value and deserve to be treated with dignity, you will always struggle in your leadership. And it will be impossible for you to be a high-road leader.

Valuing people is not about giving them compliments or making them feel important. Nor is it about getting them to like you (my problem early in my career). No, it's seeing all people's worth as human beings, letting them know you see that worth, and helping them to feel their worth and believe it themselves. If we are to take the high road, we can't pick and choose who we value. We should never devalue someone by accepting others' low opinion of them or placing a low value on them ourselves.

People can sense whether we truly value them. They know when we are sincere and genuine. They can tell when we are being phony. And they know when we devalue them. In my opinion, as a culture we lost our way when we went from simply disagreeing with others to devaluing them because we disagree. That's when we crossed the line into low-road leadership. It's one of the reasons so many people are so angry all the time. And when others take the low road with them, they become even angrier. It's always easier to make a negative point than to make a positive difference. But nobody ever wins with anger. It's a negative emotion that doesn't add value to anyone.

You may be wondering how you can value all people when you may know nothing about them. That was a question I was asked recently at a conference with the top educators of public schools from across America. They were interested in learning about the curriculum my nonprofit foundation uses to develop millions of students internationally. In roundtable settings, the curriculum teaches students to value others by choosing to embrace and live good values. Teachers in the South and Central American schools where it has been taught have seen the transformative impact it makes. And when it was tested in several South Carolina schools, teachers saw a significant decrease in disciplinary issues among students who took the course. To help the educators understand the curriculum, I not only explained it, but we also asked them to participate in one of the roundtables.

During a Q and A afterward, one of the leaders challenged my assertion that I value all people. "How can you make the claim that you value all of us, that you value me?" she asked. "You don't even know me. How is that possible?"

"I respect your question, and I want to answer it," I responded. "At the same time, I want to respect you and not offend you, so I want to ask your permission to answer you openly, because my explanation includes my faith. Would that be okay?" When she nodded, I said, "God created everyone in his image, so everyone should be valued. He values them, so I value them. When I look at the life of Jesus, I see he loved everyone unconditionally and valued everyone greatly. Even as he walked to his death, his motivation was to love broken and hurting people, not to condemn them, win arguments, or elevate himself."

> "There are no *ordinary* people. You have never talked to a mere mortal.... It is immortals whom we joke with, work with, marry, snub, and exploit." – C. S. Lewis

She seemed to accept my explanation. I wanted to communicate that since Jesus practiced high-road leadership every minute of his life, and I want to be like him, I must be willing to serve people, not focus on winning.

But you don't need to have any faith at all to acknowledge that everyone needs to feel valued. Every human being desires to feel their intrinsic worth and have someone else acknowledge it. As leadership professor and author Marilyn Gist says in her book *The Extraordinary Power of Leader Humility*, "Every human being has and needs a sense of self-worth—of dignity."[9] That includes more than our friends and family, more than those who help us and are pleasant to us. It includes people who are different from us, people from "the other side," and who treat us poorly or take advantage of us. I think C. S. Lewis may have said it best: "There are no *ordinary* people. You have never talked to a mere mortal. . . . It is immortals whom we joke with, work with, marry, snub, and exploit."[10]

Let me say one more thing about embracing the value of all people. To do it, you don't have to abandon good leadership practices. You can still be highly strategic. For example, in our effort to transform nations, my foundation works with the top 10 percent of the people in a country. We begin by teaching values to the leaders in the highest positions to promote positive transformation. Someone asked me recently, "If you value all people, why don't you start with the people who are suffering the most?" It's because we *do* value them that we start at the top. If we help the bottom 10 percent, their needs will be met and it will stop there because they aren't in a position to help others. Influence filters down, not up. However, if we reach the leaders and help them to embrace good values, which includes the value of valuing others, then they will mobilize and reach most of the remaining 90 percent. By starting with the people capable of reaching others, we are giving all the people a chance.

> Believing in people comes from seeing and acknowledging their potential.

Believe in the Potential of All People

While valuing all people comes from recognizing and embracing their worth, believing in people comes from seeing and acknowledging their potential. When you believe people can achieve, improve, be more than they are, and make a contribution to the world, you will value them and add value to them by investing in them. If you don't believe in others, why would you bother investing in them? But when you see people's potential, you try to lift them up because you want them to cultivate and improve the gifts, talents, and skills they possess.

What does this look like?

1. Express Your Belief in Them

Most people rise to the level of others' expectations for them. Jamie Kern Lima said, "In life, you don't rise to what you believe is possible. You rise to what you believe you are worthy of."[11] If you see their potential, express belief in them, and cast vision for a better future, they start taking steps toward that future.

This is why I intentionally see everyone as a "10" when I first meet them. I believe they can have a better life than they currently have. I don't believe they have to live according to the limitations others put on them—or that they put on themselves. Is everyone I meet going to be a 10? No. Is everyone I interact with going to choose the high road with me or others? Of course not. But I'm convinced my belief in people will empower more individuals to achieve and move up to the high road than if I didn't believe in them. So I choose to believe in all people. Only they can prove me wrong.

> "In life, you don't rise to what you believe is possible. You rise to what you believe you are worthy of." – *Jamie Kern Lima*

2. Equip Them

What's the greatest expression of belief in another person? Equipping them! Equipping is belief in action. When you invest in someone by teaching, training, coaching, or mentoring them, you put your time and money where your mouth is. There can be no doubt in a person's mind that you value them. Equipping is an expression of value in another person.

As you equip people, all you can offer them is what you have to give. It's up to them to take it and make the most of it. My desire is to add value to people and help them improve, but I know not everyone will take what I have to give and run with it. That's their choice. I don't feel any need to try to force anyone to receive it, nor do I feel obligated to change what I give or how I teach it. I assume whoever connects with my ideas and wants to go higher and further will benefit. And if it doesn't connect, hopefully they will find help from someone else.

3. Challenge Them

I value people and have so much faith in human potential that I believe our ability to grow is limitless. That's why I wrote the book *No Limits*. Nobody has to hit the lid of their capacity. Each of us can keep growing as long as we live. That's why I'm still dedicated to personal growth in my late seventies.

As a leader, I must at times challenge the people I lead. I need to have candid conversations with them about where they're not striving to do their best or working up to their potential. These conversations are rooted in my belief in them. If I see more in them than they see in themselves, I desire to challenge them to go to a higher level. Sometimes these conversations can be uncomfortable, but they help people to grow and change. If you lead a team, you can demonstrate your belief in your players by challenging them.

Extend Unconditional Love to All People

Dad's advice to love people unconditionally came out of his deep faith. But you don't have to possess faith like his or mine to love people. It's a choice, a mindset. It's like believing every person you meet has the potential to teach you something. Here's how it works:

VALUE ALL PEOPLE

Valuing people comes from embracing their worth.
Belief speaks to the potential you see in them.
Unconditional love accepts others with no strings attached.

Most people are capable of loving. The greater challenge is loving unconditionally. (If the word *love* seems too challenging, think of it as unconditional acceptance.) It's hard enough to love friends and family unconditionally. Extending it to difficult people is especially challenging. The best path toward loving others unconditionally is to begin by valuing people and believing in them. If you truly value and believe in people, unconditional love becomes easier—not easy, but easier.

Unconditional love is a gift, a gift that not everyone knows they need—until they receive it. And then they recognize it's the best gift they can ever receive. When you extend unconditional love, you don't devalue the person. It doesn't matter what they say or don't say, do or fail to do; you keep accepting them and caring about them with no strings attached. That mindset will always be tested, and you'll have to recommit to it time after time. But if you can continue to love people unconditionally as a leader, you create an atmosphere like no other.

HOW TO CREATE A CHANGE OF HEART

You may be thinking that this all sounds very idealistic. I agree that it is. But that doesn't mean it isn't worth striving for. Even if you're someone who doesn't naturally value people, believe in them, or unconditionally love them, you can change. And if you want to be a high-road leader, you *must* change. I know that's possible because my father, who gave me that advice, didn't start life as a naturally positive person. He worked at it. And it genuinely changed him. When he was in his nineties, he once said, "Oh, Son, isn't it great that the older you get, the more you love people?" I replied that I knew lots of individuals who didn't love people as they got older. But he did because he had made that choice and lived it every day of his life.

If you desire to value all people and become the best leader you can be on the high road, then follow these steps:

1. Develop Humble Appreciation for Yourself

How do you think about yourself? The answer to this question is key to understanding your mindset toward other people. High-road leaders who value people have a strong, healthy sense of self-worth, yet at the same time they are humble, meaning they don't think too much of themselves or *about* themselves too much. Marilyn Gist calls this quality "leader humility" and defines it as "a tendency to *feel* and *display* a deep regard for others' dignity."[12] Possessing the humility to give others respect and honor simply because they are human beings is vital to leading on the high road.

> **How you see yourself translates to how you treat other people.**

How can leaders develop this kind of humble appreciation for themselves? Gist says, "Humility requires self-awareness and free will (choice). If people have the right foundation (the elements being reasonable self-awareness and openness to growth in this), there is a good chance they can develop or improve leader humility. If one or the other element is lacking, the odds are not good."[13]

Let's start with self-awareness. How aware are you of your attitude toward yourself? To value all people, you must believe in your own worth. How you see yourself translates to how you treat other people. Do you like yourself? Do you value yourself, believe in yourself, and accept yourself for who you are?

At the same time, while seeing worth in yourself, you must recognize you're not worth more than anyone else. You must recognize that you have value, but don't use it to elevate yourself. Instead, you must use it to elevate others.

Mark Cole, the CEO of my companies, worked with an employee, Fred, who unintentionally devalued people. He wasn't mean or nasty; he was indifferent. He saw people according to their function or usefulness to the organization rather than seeing them as individual human beings with intrinsic value. He wasn't even aware he saw people that way.

> I love this single-word definition of leadership: *others*.

Mark had to help him develop self-awareness and work with him to improve the way he treated people. Raising his self-awareness made him a better leader. Self-awareness will help you too.

2. Choose to Start Putting Your Focus on Others

I recently read an article by my friend Sam Chand. I love what he wrote about leadership: "In an age characterized by narcissistic and hubris-driven leaders, a focus on *others* is refreshing." In fact, I love Sam's single-word definition of leadership: *others*. He went on explain that to him, it meant focusing on others, serving others, and investing in others.[14] I couldn't agree more.

If you desire to improve yourself, your relationships with others, and your leadership, you must make a choice. You must consciously start putting your focus on others. You must want to better yourself and travel the high road. If you are willing to change to become someone who values all people, it will not only transform your leadership; it will transform your life.

3. Take Action

A vital part of the process of change is taking action. A change in behavior helps to create a change in heart. Most people need to act their way into feeling to create lasting change. If they wait for the feeling to come, they never get where they want or need to go. If you need to change, do it through behavior. You must *show* people through your actions that you value them. If you already care about people and value them, but you don't take action to express it, how will they know?

What actions can you take to let people know you value them? Start with these:

- Acknowledge them with kind words.
- Seek common ground with them by asking questions.
- Look for value in them and express it to them.
- Find ways to add value to them.
- Treat them with dignity.

Valuing people is an intentional action. You must choose to value others and add value to them. It doesn't happen without an act of will.

4. Allow Your Heart for People to Grow

Going through the process of valuing people can help you grow to where you genuinely value them. Charlie Wetzel, my book-writing partner for nearly thirty years, says he has always been more focused on tasks than people, and he found it necessary to change his mindset to become a better leader and a better person. He found that taking action helped him to change in a major way. In his thirties, he was asked to coach small group leaders. Charlie has a heart for teaching and developing people. He knew from studying my 5 Levels of Leadership that if he wanted to get the chance to develop people, he needed to get their permission to lead them by building relationships. So what did he do? He is a highly strategic and productive person, so he made connecting with his leaders a task on his to-do list. He scheduled regular lunches with each of the leaders he was coaching to get to know them, find common ground, and build relationships with them. By doing that, he earned trust. But something else happened. By making the effort to get to know people, he started to appreciate that everybody has a story and everybody has challenges in their life they're trying to overcome. His empathy increased and he developed a greater heart for people.

"There was a particular leader I was asked to coach whom I didn't especially like," says Charlie. "But I went into the relationship treating him with respect and dignity and worked to get to know him. I ended up loving the guy."

Changing your actions to show people you value them may start out feeling like duty. At first you may take positive action to value someone and think, *OK, I got that out of the way. Now I can get back to work.* But my hope is that season won't last long and you will experience a change in heart and not have to keep going through the motions. But no matter what, it's important to keep taking action, because without it, you won't change.

5. Enjoy the Positive Return

High-road leaders don't value people to get a reward. That's not the right motivation. However, there is eventually a return for valuing people. It comes with time and consistency. I've found three kinds of returns you can receive by valuing others:

- **A Relational Return:** When you value all people, you can't help but build better relationships. You open doors to new relationships with every interaction, and you improve relationships with individuals with whom you're already acquainted.

- **An Emotional Return:** I've never known a person who values others and adds value to them not to receive an emotional return from doing it. Few things in life are more rewarding than helping another human being.
- **A Leadership Return:** Valuing people also has a return for you as a leader. When you care about people, value them, and act in their best interest, your influence increases because they trust you and have a greater desire to work with you. And even if there isn't a direct connection with you on your team or in your organization, they will want to help you succeed or connect you to people who can help you directly.

When you value all people, everybody wins.

The ability to value all people by believing in them, caring about them, and unconditionally accepting and loving them comes from having the right perspective. The secret is in how you see others. How we view things is how we do things. The right mindset comes from recognizing the world is not about you. It's about others. It's a choice every person can make and that every leader *must* make to travel on the high road. Only you can take ownership of the process. You know the steps, but nobody can take them for you. I hope you take them because valuing people will open the door to all the other steps you must take to live and lead on the high road.

> How we view things is how we do things.

The Pathway to Valuing All People:
SELF-WORTH

If you have trouble embracing the idea that all people have value and should be valued by you, it may be because people haven't valued you the way they should have. Maybe you haven't been shown respect by the people most important to you. Maybe others have not regarded your dignity.

As I mentioned earlier, I was fortunate to have experienced unconditional love from my mother that made me very secure in my self-worth. If you didn't receive this kind of love, first let me say I'm sorry. I'm sorry you didn't receive the love and respect you deserve.

Second, let me be the one to tell you this: ***you have great value.*** You have great worth just because of who you are, regardless of what you have or have not done in your life. You don't need to be more talented than you already are. You don't have to achieve anything great. You don't have to earn love and respect. Because you are a human being, you matter. You matter to me. You matter to God. You matter to others in this world.

Let that soak in. Embrace it. Allow yourself to feel it down deep to your core. Not only will it help you to be yourself and follow your path as a human being and leader; it will make it easier for you to value others. You will want them to experience the same dignity and self-worth you do because you know what a difference it can make.

3

ACKNOWLEDGE YOUR HUMANNESS

As I entered my midthirties, I was experiencing extraordinary success. Margaret and I had been married for fifteen years, our relationship was strong, and we had two beautiful children. After lots of work, my communication skills had gone to a new level, and I was in demand as a speaker. I was starting to be recognized as an authority on leadership and had begun to develop a national profile. And the three churches I'd led during my career had grown dramatically, with my current one being recognized as among the ten largest in America. My confidence was high, and I believed ever-greater days were ahead of me.

At that time, I met regularly with a mentor. At lunch one day, my mentor looked at me and said, "John, everyone is constantly praising you these days. A lot of people are telling you how amazing you are. But I need to tell you something: you're not amazing. Your gift is amazing, but you are not. You're one step from stupid."

He went on to explain to me that the gifts we have are always greater than the person. Whatever talents or gifts we possess were given to us. We didn't earn them. We don't deserve them. We can take no credit for them. If our gifts are great, they don't make us better than anyone else, nor does our possession of them excuse poor behavior. The best we can do is use whatever we have been given to benefit others.

For the first time I understood that when people experienced something that comes from my giftedness, they could mistakenly attribute it to me. I realized I needed to separate my self-worth from my abilities. If I didn't, I could lose perspective, and I might begin to believe I'm as good as my talent, when I'm not. It's dangerous to think more of yourself than you should. Because my mentor challenged me and helped me acknowledge my humanness, I shifted my thinking and put more emphasis on the good choices I made than the gifts I had been given. And that has helped me a lot, because acknowledging our humanness is essential to high-road living.

> "There is an eagle in me that wants to soar, and there is a hippopotamus in me that wants to wallow in the mud."
> – Attributed to Carl Sandburg

THE EAGLE AND THE HIPPOPOTAMUS

There's a quote, often attributed to Carl Sandburg, that is an insightful description of our condition as human beings. It says, "There is an eagle in me that wants to soar, and there is a hippopotamus in me that wants to wallow in the mud."[15] I find this to be true. The eagle in me makes me want to rise up and do great things. Unfortunately, it also makes me want to look down on others. I want to judge them by their actions and results while I want to give myself the benefit of the doubt based on my intentions and feelings.

Many years ago, I came across a piece that shows how we tend to think about ourselves and others:

> When the other person takes a long time, he's slow.
> When I take a long time, I'm thorough.
> When the other person doesn't do it, he's lazy.
> When I don't do it, I'm busy.

ACKNOWLEDGE YOUR HUMANNESS

When the other person doesn't follow the rules, he's rude.
When I don't follow the rules, I'm original.
When the other person gets ahead, he gets the lucky breaks.
When I manage to get ahead, I'm smart and hardworking.[16]

That's why it's wise to also remember the hippopotamus in us. It reminds me that all of us like to wallow. Everyone has experienced days that we hope nobody else ever finds out about. I've had them. Haven't you?

We're all flawed human beings. We're all one step from stupid. If I acknowledge the hippo in me, then whenever I see someone else in the mud, I am liable to think, *I can relate, because I've been there!* When I see others' shortcomings, I can see my own shortcomings. I think of my failures as being similar to their failures. I recognize my poor attitude is no better or worse than their poor attitude. We're all in this together. Knowing that makes me less likely to judge them and more likely to give them grace and lend them a hand. In other words, I will be more likely to take the high road.

To be a high-road person, I must learn to give grace to myself and others instead of being critical or unkind. Take a look at what results, depending on how we view ourselves and others:

Treatment of Self	Treatment of Others	I May Become a
Judge Myself Harshly	Judge Others Harshly	Cynic
Judge Myself Harshly	Give Grace to Others	Doormat
Give Grace to Myself	Judge Others Harshly	Narcissist
Give Grace to Myself	Give Grace to Others	High-Road Person

Acknowledging my humanness leads me to the conclusion that I am no better than others. I'm a flawed human just like they are. At the same time, I'm also no worse than others because they are just as flawed as I am. Therefore, I should not think too much of myself or too little of myself. Recognizing our humanity allows us to create common ground with others. If I remember that and treat people accordingly, I have the potential to be a high-road leader.

IF YOU SEEM TO BE STUCK IN THE MUD

I should pause here and say that acknowledging your humanness can be a very difficult process for some people. Many people today feel depressed and have a difficult time dealing with their shortcomings and negative feelings. According to Gallup, the percentage of adults who say they have been diagnosed with depression at some point in their lifetime is 29 percent.[17] Experts in the mental health field identify depression as one of the most prevalent mental health conditions in the United States and say it is the leading cause of disability worldwide.[18] This sense of discouragement causes some people to beat themselves up when they think about their flaws.

I admit that I have difficulty relating to people who feel this way. However, I do have empathy for them. I found the thought patterns of depressed people that Kristin Neff shared in her book *Self-Compassion: The Proven Power of Being Kind to Yourself* to be eye-opening:

> All my life I've been depressed. I've always felt like there was something wrong with me and that I was stupid and ugly and gross. I want to have more friends but I can't figure out how to do it. . . . I don't say things out in public much because I might say something stupid and someone will laugh at me and humiliate me.[19]

If this describes how you feel, I wish I could help you personally. I hope the rest of this chapter encourages you. But if you've been stuck in the mud for a long time, I advise you to get help from a professional who can help you understand how valuable you really are. Please speak to someone about how you feel. And seek assistance from someone who has been trained to walk with you through your challenges. I believe in you and know you can come out on the other side of this experience with your head above water. You can come to a place where you enjoy life and add value to others on the high road.

HOW TO ACKNOWLEDGE AND ACCEPT YOUR HUMANNESS

What is my best advice to people for acknowledging their humanness without becoming discouraged or discounting their ability to lead others effectively? I recommend that you do five things:

1. See Yourself

The first and most important step in acknowledging your humanness is developing self-awareness. How can you acknowledge your humanness unless you know who you are? In recent years, I've been given the opportunity to work with some of the best songwriters in Nashville to get their help writing songs based on the themes in my books. A song I wrote with Bobby Hamrick, Chris August, and James Slater is called "Get Over Myself." I love the chorus:

> I've got to find myself
> To know myself
> To be myself
> To improve myself
> To get over myself
> So I can give myself to you.

Notice that the beginning of the process of being someone who can add value to others is self-awareness: finding and knowing ourselves.

What does it mean to be self-aware and to be able to see yourself clearly? It begins with understanding our strengths, weaknesses, feelings, thoughts, and values. This can be difficult, but when we can, it opens new possibilities for us, as this story illustrates:

> A wise woman traveling in the mountains found a precious stone in a stream. The next day, she met another traveler who said he was hungry, and the wise woman opened her bag to share her food. The hungry traveler saw the precious stone and asked the woman to give it to him. She did so without hesitation. The traveler left, rejoicing in his good fortune. He knew the stone was worth enough to give him security for a lifetime. But a few days later he came back to return the stone to the wise woman.
>
> "I've been thinking," he said. "I know how valuable this stone is, but I give it back in the hope that you will give me something even more precious. Give me what you have within you that enabled you to give me the stone."[20]

In that moment, the traveler saw himself and wanted to change.

Seeing yourself clearly also requires the ability to recognize how you affect the people around you.[21] Organizational psychologist, researcher, and *New York Times* bestselling author Tasha Eurich calls these two sides of the same coin internal and external self-awareness, and she says that acquiring one does not automatically mean we acquire the other. Yet both are necessary if we want to lead effectively. Eurich writes,

Research suggests that when we see ourselves clearly, we are more confident and more creative. We make sounder decisions, build stronger relationships, and communicate more effectively. We're less likely to lie, cheat, and steal. We are better workers who get more promotions. And we're more-effective leaders with more-satisfied employees and more-profitable companies.[22]

In other words, every one of the qualities and abilities we need to lead on the high road is enhanced by self-awareness.

As you work to see yourself clearly and become more self-aware, beware of three common obstacles you may need to overcome:

> It's hard to listen and learn when you think you already know everything.

Experience

It would be natural to believe that the more experience a person has, the greater their self-awareness, but the opposite is often true. Eurich points out, "Studies have shown that people do not always learn from experience, that expertise does not help people root out false information, and that seeing ourselves as highly experienced can keep us from doing our homework, seeking disconfirming evidence, and questioning our assumptions."[23] It's hard to listen and learn when you think you already know everything.

Power

Studies also show the more power a leader holds, the more likely they are to overestimate their skills and abilities. This may occur because leaders stop listening or because people stop challenging their thinking. Employees below them may be afraid to speak up, and at higher levels, leaders have fewer people above them in the organization to give them constructive feedback.[24]

Pride

If we possess too much pride and are trying to feed our egos, we are less likely to recognize our weaknesses and are more likely to overinflate our strengths. Both make us less aware. Instead, we need to embrace humility. Jim Weber, CEO of Brooks Running, said, "There's nothing weak about humility in leadership. It's actually a sign of confidence."[25]

> "There's nothing weak about humility in leadership. It's actually a sign of confidence." – Jim Weber

The best way to combat these potential problems is to seek out honest feedback from people with your best interest at heart who are willing to tell you the truth. If you're willing to listen to them and take in their observations without being defensive, you can come to see yourself more realistically, and that's necessary for the next step in acknowledging your humanness.

2. Care for Yourself

What should you do when you receive all this negative information about yourself? Too many people beat themselves up. Instead, care for yourself by practicing self-compassion. Kristin Neff, who literally wrote the book on the subject, said, "Self-compassion is treating yourself with the same kindness, care and concern you show a loved one. We need to frame it in terms of humanity. That's what makes self-compassion so different: 'I'm an imperfect human being living an imperfect life.'"[26]

The most important voice in your life is your own. Every day you say things to yourself. How would you describe that inner voice? Is it kind, understanding, and empathetic? Or is it hard, critical, and demanding? If you don't show yourself kindness, how will you extend it to anyone else? As Broadway actor and singer Kristin Chenoweth said, "If you can learn to love yourself and all the flaws, you can love other people so much better."

I do this by being my own best friend. I love and care for myself. When I'm the hippo in the mud, I don't scold myself. I'm human, so I don't expect to always be the eagle. So I encourage myself. And I invite myself to get out of the mud because the hippo isn't really who I am.

Author, speaker, and entrepreneur Ron Dube says, "Self-compassion isn't about letting yourself off the hook for difficult emotions and mistakes, or giving into your every whim. It's about acknowledging the tough parts of life, and giving yourself the love you need to keep going."[27] Pay attention to your experiences, and when you fall short, acknowledge the fact but don't put yourself down for it. Instead, encourage yourself and find a positive way forward.

Experts say one of the ways to do this is to ask *what* instead of *why* about our mistakes and shortcomings. Asking *why* tends to lead us into unproductive negative thoughts, and if we don't have the means to understand why, we make things up to explain our feelings. That

> "If you can learn to love yourself and all the flaws, you can love other people so much better." – *Kristin Chenoweth*

doesn't help us. On the other hand, *what* questions help us to be objective, future-focused, and inclined to action, which can help us improve.[28]

For example, let's say you put a lot of time and energy into launching an important new initiative. And it fails. Will it help if you ask yourself, *Why did I fail? Why did I make those choices? Why didn't it work?* Instead, ask, *What went wrong? What went right? What can I do next time to make this better?* These questions put you on a better path for dealing with the problem and toward improving yourself and your current situation.

3. Forgive Yourself

Seeing yourself clearly makes you aware of all the places you fall short in life—your weaknesses, failures, and struggles. Measuring those characteristics against an unrealistic standard can be profoundly discouraging. Unfortunately, doing that has become increasingly common and has heightened our tendency toward perfectionism. Author, speaker, and psychologist Stephanie Harrison observed,

> Studies show that perfectionism has significantly increased over the last two decades, to a dangerous effect. Young people hold unrealistic standards for themselves as well as those around them.... Internalizing such idealism negatively affects everyone, but especially younger generations who are likely to be more depressed, more burned out, and less productive than the generations before them. The same research also highlights that perfectionism is a leading cause of increased anxiety and depression among young people in the US, the UK, and Canada.[29]

The solution to this tendency is forgiveness. You must let go of perfectionism and forgive yourself for not being perfect.

Everyone has flaws. And that's not only okay; it's normal. As Confucius said, "Better a diamond with a flaw than a pebble without." Pretending you don't have flaws only makes you unaware or inauthentic. Ignoring your shortcomings or lying to yourself about them doesn't help you either. Acknowledging them and forgiving yourself for them improves your outlook toward yourself, reduces internal stress, boosts your empathy toward others, and makes you *better* at improving yourself because you view your shortcomings more objectively and realistically.[30]

4. Laugh at Yourself

When you can forgive yourself for not being perfect, it becomes easy to get over yourself and begin to laugh at yourself. Few things do more to help a person live a healthier life, build connections with others, and improve their leadership. According to marketing and business-development executive Anne Gherini,

> Research suggests that a tangible way to spot a self-aware leader is by looking for a self-deprecating sense of humor. People that can admit to their failures or shortcomings with a smile are more approachable. Some may think that admitting to failures or faults reveals vulnerability, but really the best leaders must constantly judge their own capabilities, as well as those of others. They must understand when they need help and proactively surround themselves with people that excel where they fall short.
>
> Being so comfortable and confident that you can laugh at yourself builds trust within a team. Leaders with this magical combination of confidence and self-awareness bond more tightly with teammates by de-emphasizing the differences in status between themselves and their employees.[31]

> "Research suggests that a tangible way to spot a self-aware leader is by looking for a self-deprecating sense of humor." – *Anne Gherini*

I find it easy to laugh at myself because I have so many foibles, and I am always doing silly things. I'm constantly losing things. I'm such a klutz that I knock over glasses at the table and spill on myself all the time. And I'm the most technologically illiterate person I know. The list of my shortcomings is so long, all I can do is laugh.

I also love to use self-deprecating humor when I communicate and when I lead others. Nothing takes down barriers like a joke at our own expense. It lets everyone know that *we* know we're fallible and imperfect. Because we don't take ourselves too seriously, no one else is expected to either. So go ahead: laugh at yourself—everyone else is.

There is no downside to laughing at yourself. Citing work by psychologist and humor researcher Arnie Cann, Cindy Lamothe writes, "Laughter releases dopamine, increases blood flow, and strengthens the heart, but beyond its many health perks, a good sense of humor leads to increased optimism, which in turn, boosts our resiliency and enables us to thrive when we're faced with adversity. Cann believes that simply having this awareness of how humor can improve our lives can eventually lead to greater well-being."[32] So if you want to live well and lead others on the high road, laugh!

5. Believe in Yourself

Once you see yourself, care for yourself, forgive yourself, and laugh at yourself, you're ready to reap the greatest internal benefit of acknowledging your humanness, and that is cultivating confident humility. Author and professor Adam Grant writes,

> Confidence and humility are often seen as opposites. But if you reflect on the leaders you admire most, chances are that they embody both of these qualities in tandem....
>
> Confident humility is being secure enough in your expertise and strengths to admit your ignorance and weaknesses. . . . Confidence without humility breeds blind arrogance, and humility without confidence yields debilitating

doubt. Confident humility allows you to believe in yourself while questioning your strategies.[33]

If you are able to acknowledge your humanness and develop confident humility, you will place yourself in a position to be a high-road leader who treats people well and accomplishes much.

Grant suggests three steps a leader can take to develop or strengthen their confident humility. I'll summarize them here:

Become Part of a Learning Culture

When an environment is focused on competition, then winning becomes paramount and individuals are reluctant to admit fault or show weakness. In contrast, an environment that values learning invites people to acknowledge what they don't know, test ideas, challenge assumptions, and make mistakes.

Early in my journey as a leader, I became aware of the value of a positive learning environment. Recognizing this, I wrote a description to help me create one in my organization. Positive learning environments have the following characteristics:

> Others are ahead of us.
> We are continually challenged.
> Our focus is forward.
> The atmosphere is affirming.
> We are out of our comfort zone.
> We wake up excited.
> Failure is not our enemy.
> Everyone is growing.
> We desire change.
> Growth is expected.

If it is in your power to create a growth environment for yourself and others, then do so. If it's not, then seek out someplace with a learning culture and tap into it, using it to help you develop humble confidence.

Give Yourself the Benefit of Doubt

I love this idea from Grant. He suggests not that we give ourselves *the benefit of the doubt,* meaning we would assume we may be right. No, he recommends that *doubting ourselves* offers us a benefit. He writes, "When you question your knowledge and strategies, you become motivated to seek out new insights, which can broaden and deepen your learning."[34]

> "When you question your knowledge and strategies, you become motivated to seek out new insights, which can broaden and deepen your learning." – Adam Grant

This is an incredible way to acknowledge your humanness and gain leadership confidence at the same time. If you adopt a beginner's mindset instead of an expert's, and embrace an attitude of willingness to be questioned and instructed, not only will you gain quiet confidence, but the people who work with you will gain confidence in you and your leadership.

Identify Where You May Be Wrong

Finally, Grant believes identifying pieces of information or opinions that conflict with what we believe can curb the overconfidence many leaders often display. His two favorite questions for himself are, *How do you know?* and *What if we're wrong?* Finding even a single reason we're wrong can help us remain appropriately humble.

And here's what's really interesting: accepting our humanness and possessing humble confidence does nothing to diminish our leadership ability. In a study of medical students, those who possessed doubts about their ability were just as effective in diagnosing illnesses as their more confident counterparts. Furthermore, the more humble students rated higher in bedside manner, empathy, respect, and professionalism.[35]

Neurologist John Noseworthy, who served as president and CEO of the Mayo Clinic, said,

> People who don't have insight into their behavior are very difficult to change. People who have humility are generally sensitive to how they interact with others. So, we select for it, and we also train for it, through feedback and coaching. We need people with self-awareness and humility who are open to criticism and guidance. If they lack that openness, they won't be very successful in leadership.[36]

High-road leaders are aware of their humanness. When you're aware of your humanness and you acknowledge you don't know all the answers, you listen to yourself and others. You better understand yourself and others. You develop empathy for yourself and others and care for them. And you are better able to lead yourself and others on the high road.

> **When you're aware of your humanness and you acknowledge you don't know all the answers, you listen to yourself and others.**

You may have to do some work to accept your own humanness and extend grace to yourself first, but you can do it. None of us wants to be judged by our worst days. I certainly don't. If you judge me by my worst days, I shouldn't be writing a book. I shouldn't be speaking. I'm disqualified. I desire grace and acceptance. So do you. So does everyone else in this world. We can learn to give it—as mothers and fathers, as friends and neighbors, and as leaders.

Pathway to Acknowledging Your Humanness:
SELF-AWARENESS

Most of us believe we are self-aware. However, researchers have found few people are truly self-aware—only one or two individuals out of ten.[37] That means it's more than 80 percent likely you are *not* self-aware.

How can you change that? Start by answering some questions. These will help you with internal self-awareness:

- How well do you know your strengths? Do you know what gifts and abilities you possess that set you apart from others?
- How about your weaknesses and flaws? Do you know what they are? Are you realistic about them? More importantly, are you honest and open about them?
- What about your feelings? How aware are you of them? How do you react in response to challenges, opposition, indifference, failure, and conflict? How do you handle success?
- Have you identified your values? Have you thought through what you *would* and *would not* do in support of them?

Equally important to your development of self-awareness is being conscious of how people respond to you. Answer these questions:

ACKNOWLEDGE YOUR HUMANNESS

- When you interact with people, do they find you overly talkative, aloof, aggressive, condescending, abrupt, kind, transactional?
- When things go wrong, how do people react to *your* reaction? In general, are you liked or disliked, sought out or avoided?

Knowing how others experience you is another key to unlocking your leadership.

The more self-aware you become, the easier it will be for you to be yourself and take the high road with others.

4

DO THE RIGHT THINGS FOR THE RIGHT REASONS

I CAN TELL YOU THE DAY I REALLY LEARNED HIGH-ROAD LEADERSHIP. It was when I was a junior in college. I was a student at Circleville Bible College (now Ohio Christian University), where my father served as president. I still lived at home because, well, why would I want to live in a dorm when Mom would take care of me, and I could eat her home-cooked meals? Dad had been leading the college for about four years by then, and I knew it was presenting challenges to him. Sometimes I overheard him talking to my mother about it. Plus, Dad was getting migraine headaches, which often happened when he was under great pressure.

Dad was a good leader, and he was accomplishing fantastic things as he worked to create a great school. But the board he was required to work with caused him terrible problems. Three board members treated him horribly. They resented him because his success had far surpassed their own. And they worked against Dad because he prioritized making genuine progress over preserving hollow tradition. Another two board members usually went along with those three. While that meant only five of the people actively worked against him, they planned and coordinated their attacks and did everything in their power to make Dad's job difficult.

A LIFE-CHANGING EXPERIENCE

I didn't realize how bad things were until one night in the college library. Because Mom was the college librarian and had the keys, she would allow me to use them after hours to get away from people and study there. One night I was alone working on a paper when I thought I heard someone talking. I got up and crept toward where the sound was coming from, and I discovered it was my father. I watched quietly from the other side of a bookshelf as he paced back and forth talking to God. He was angry and frustrated and hurt. He was laying out all the horrendous things that had been done to him in a board meeting earlier that night, and he was actually weeping.

The anger rose up in me as Dad poured his heart out. But then his posture changed. He stopped walking, went down onto his knees, and then lay face-down on the floor. And his prayers went to another level. I could hear him asking God to forgive them and to bless their lives. As I slipped away quietly, I thought, *That's the kind of leader I want to become.*

I didn't tell my dad that I had heard him, but a few days later I did sit down with him and Mom to ask if I could go talk to the board. In my twenty-year-old arrogance, I wanted to challenge their motives and believed I could straighten out their actions. I was convinced if they knew how wonderful a man and how good a leader Dad was, it would solve all the problems.

"No, John," my dad replied. "That's not the way we do leadership here. If you're a Maxwell, you have to take the high road."

I knew Dad could have pushed those five men out. He could have been political, working the other ten people to outmaneuver them. I wanted him to, but that would have violated his values. His motives were pure. He wanted to improve the college and create the best environment for students to get a great education. Even though it would cost him, even though the board members would not work with him, even though he would have been justified in retaliating, he did what he believed was right.

I learned a valuable lesson from that experience with my dad, and it changed me. Many times growing up I had heard him say we should take the high road with others. It was something I could parrot back. It was something I believed in. But that night I saw him as just a man alone, desperately talking to God about what was happening to him, yet forgiving others and treating them well. He wasn't acting. He wasn't playing parent for my benefit. He didn't even know I was there. I went from thinking, *I ought to be a high-road leader* to *I want to be a high-road leader*. It made me hungry to be that kind of person.

I also learned something else. I told myself, *You don't have to win every time. Just do the right things for the right reasons.* I was young, inexperienced, and highly competitive. Seeing my father forgive instead of fight began to change my thinking. How many leaders end up going down the low road because they feel they have to win every time? Seeing the way Dad forgave them inspired me. It helped me realize I don't always need to win, but I do always need to forgive.

> I don't always need to win, but I do always need to forgive.

Dad worked as president of the college for a total of seventeen years. Over time, those negative people left the board, and that made his job easier. And here is what's interesting. The last time Dad and I were speakers together at an event many years later, one of those low-road former board members was in attendance. After we were done, he approached Dad and asked for his forgiveness. And my father said, "Absolutely. All is forgiven." They hugged one another. The man looked relieved because he had carried the burden of his wrong motives for more than forty years. But Dad hadn't carried that weight. He had acted with good motives and had forgiven the man decades before.

MOTIVES MATTER

When I was a child, my parents taught me to do the right thing with the right attitude. They cared about what I did *and* why I did it. That instilled in me the understanding that our motives always matter. That's especially true for leaders.

The most important question leaders can ask themselves is: *Why do I want to lead others?* In other words, what are my motives? What are my reasons for doing what I do? Are they open or hidden? Am I doing it because I have a personal agenda or desire personal gain? Or am I doing it for the benefit of others? I think we all have the innate belief that we *should* help one another, but our motives often cause us to resist doing the right thing, even when we know we should.

When politician Rahm Emanuel was chief of staff for President Obama, he said, "You never want a serious crisis to go to waste.... It's an opportunity to do things that you think you could not do before."[38] What he meant was that you can use it to get your way and push your own agenda. This, unfortunately, seems to be the attitude of many political and cultural leaders today. Instead of seeing problems and tragedies as chances to practice high-road leadership, rally people together, and give their best efforts to creating solutions that are good for everyone, they leverage a crisis to divide people and pontificate about how much better they are than the other side. Why would any leader go out of the way to divide people? There's only one reason. They have a personal agenda. That is an issue of motives.

The last time national leaders came together during a crisis and worked to serve the common good was in the weeks immediately after the tragedy of 9/11. Democrats and Republicans, southerners

> The most important question leaders can ask themselves is: *Why do I want to lead others?*

and northerners, rich and poor, urbanites, suburbanites, and country folk all worked together with common goals. Unfortunately, the unity and cooperation didn't last long because it did not serve the agendas of the party leaders, and soon they were dividing people once again. Today, even when some leaders appear to be cooperating with others, they're actually acting like the small child who was told to sit in the corner as punishment for something he'd done. The whole time he's thinking, *I'm sitting down on the outside, but I'm standing up on the inside.*

Leaders who don't do the right thing need to check their motives. Some leaders purposely devalue people, divide them, and exploit them because their motives are selfish. Others are unaware that they are harming people through their actions because their motives are driven by pain, emptiness, insecurity, or some other internal cause. They may have no idea what they're doing isn't right.

"What's *right*?" you may ask. It's doing what benefits the majority of the people. It's wanting what's best for yourself *and* others. It's following the Golden Rule: do unto others as you would have them do unto you. That's the standard, but it's hard to live by. I know I have to check my own motives frequently so I don't drift off course into low-road leadership. Any time I'm trying to move others solely for my own benefit, I'm off course. Anything that's not serving others at least as much as it's serving me is manipulation. I may try to convince myself that I'm motivating people, but I'm not. Take a look at the differences:

Motivation	Manipulation
Is for Mutual Advantage	Is for My Advantage
Cares About Results and the People	Cares Only About Results
Is Fueled by Love	Is Fueled by Ego
Relies on Substance	Relies on Style
Empowers People	Controls People

Values People	Devalues People
Fosters Loyalty	Fosters Resentment
Takes the High Road	Takes the Low Road

One of the things all leaders have in common is their ability to see *more* than others see and *before* others see. This *more and before* ability gives them a distinct advantage. I'll talk more about this in chapter 10. As leaders, we need to think about what we intend to do with this knowledge. Will we use it to benefit ourselves or others? If we intend to use it to serve ourselves, our motives are unhealthy. When our motives are healthy, we use it to serve others.

> "A man of character will make himself worthy of any position he is given." – *Mahatma Gandhi*

Do you know *why* you want to lead others? Do you know *why* you do what you do when you interact with people? What drives you?

- Are you trying to climb the ladder to advance your career?
- Are you working to gain power so that you can be free to do what you want?
- Are you seeking recognition, validation, honor, or fame?
- Are you motived by financial gain and the status it brings?
- Are you pursuing happiness, comfort, freedom, or pleasure?

If you're doing any of these at the expense of other people, your motives are leading you down the low road instead of the high road in your leadership. If you want to be a good leader, you need to change. And here's the good news: you can. You can improve your motives by working on your character. You can start making choices based on good values. As Mahatma Gandhi said, "A man of character will make himself worthy of any position he is given."[39]

THE RIGHT VALUES HELP YOU STOP MAKING WRONG CHOICES

To help you begin making the right choices, I want to encourage you to reject some actions that will undermine your leadership:

1. Stop Chasing What's Easy

Doing the right things for the right reasons can be challenging. It often goes against the grain. The pathway to high-road leadership is an uphill climb. That shouldn't be a surprise because everything worthwhile in life is uphill. Unfortunately, most of us have uphill hopes but downhill habits, so we have to work to break them and develop new ways of thinking and acting.

How do you get started? Stop doing what's easy. Nobel Prize–winning scientist Marie Curie said, "I was taught that the way of progress was neither swift nor easy."[40] Doing what's easy is a selfish choice. What's easy for you is rarely what's best for others. It's often not even best for you! The right choice is always the choice that's best for everyone, no matter how difficult it is.

> **The pathway to high-road leadership is an uphill climb.**

2. Stop Chasing Applause

When I was a boy, my father gave me Dale Carnegie's *How to Win Friends and Influence People* to read. It made such a strong impression on me, I reread it three more times while I was in high school. One of the things Carnegie addressed was people's desire for recognition. He said, "It is what Freud calls 'the desire to be great.' It is what Dewey calls 'the desire to be important.'" He went on to quote William James: "The deepest principle in human nature is the craving to be appreciated."[41]

This desire for applause can drive you right off the high road. The thirst for fame, promotion, and credit can cause a person to cut corners or step on others to feel fulfilled. Performance coach and author Steve Magness wrote about how seeking self-worth from outside of ourselves can undermine performance and improvement. He observed, "When our self-worth is dependent on outside factors, we have what researchers call a contingent self-worth. We derive our sense of self from what people think and how we are judged. We give over control to external factors. When we utilize idle praise and combine that with undeserved rewards, we create an environment ripe for developing contingent self-worth."[42] If you seek approval from others, you're never satisfied, and the kind of self-worth Magness described is fragile and easily crushed.

In contrast, when your motivation is to do the right things for the right reasons, you are rewarded by a sense of worth and well-being that comes from within. That kind of self-esteem is stable and not easily shaken. It doesn't require external validation, and even if the choices you make invite criticism or derision from others, it remains strong. In the end, if we are motivated by applause, we care too much about what others think about us, but if we're motivated by adding value to people, we care about what others think about themselves.

3. Stop Insisting You're Right

In the wake of the death of George Floyd in Minneapolis on May 25, 2020, the nation took sides and protests erupted around the country. People who sided with the protestors were adamant that their perspective was right and were vocal about it. People who sided against the protestors were adamant that their perspective was right and were vocal about it. All both sides wanted to do was prove their rightness and the other side's wrongness, but their arguments got them nowhere with one another.

The problem with arguing loudly that *you are right* is that you're not listening and learning so that you can find out *what actually is right*.

It's the height of arrogance to believe you know everything there is to know about a subject, that you have looked at it from every angle, and that you possess the only valid perspective.

When many influential people began making statements in response to the conflict, some of my certified coaches asked me to put out a public statement about where I stood on race, but I declined. I believe my whole life is my statement. If you want to know where I stand, look at how I have treated people my entire life. I'm far from perfect, but I always try to value *all* people. However, I also sensed that I didn't truly understand the protests. It was clear to me that a police officer kneeling on Floyd's neck until he died was a terrible wrong. At the same time, I didn't understand why so many people were protesting and doing it so violently. My perception was that they were reacting too strongly to a single incident.

> The problem with arguing loudly that *you are right* is that you're not listening and learning so that you can find out *what actually is right*.

I suspected I was missing something. While the protesters' world wasn't my world, I did want to understand it, so I knew I needed to start listening. I started talking with Black friends and asking them questions about their own experiences. Every person I talked to had stories of being singled out, pulled over, and treated as "less" specifically because they were Black. That's when I finally started to grasp the bigger problem I'd been missing. Because I wanted to keep learning more about racism and injustice from another perspective, I started reading books. I began to get a glimpse of the problem and the frustrations of a whole group of people. That made me more empathetic and less judgmental.

To take the high road as a leader, we need to become good listeners. Any time we fight for our point of view and stand on how "right" we are, we will probably end up on the low road. To check ourselves, professor Matthew D. Kim suggests, "We can inventory our friendships over the past two or three years and ask ourselves, *Have I lost friends on account of 'being right'? Will I choose relationships over rightness going forward?*"[43] If we place a higher value on issues than we do on the human beings we're interacting with, we are probably off course. We need to stop trying to *be* right and understand what *is* right.

4. Stop Paying Lip Service

Have you noticed the big trend in our culture for people to make public statements about almost any issue? When a tragedy occurs, a divisive comment is made by a high-profile person, or a controversial event takes place, leaders are pushed to make a statement. Celebrities are expected to post their opinions for or against every issue. But here's the problem with that: a statement doesn't actually *do* anything other than accentuate the divide between people and their groups. Paying lip service to gain the good graces of the crowd doesn't actually serve anyone—except maybe the statement maker.

> **We need to stop trying to *be* right and understand what *is* right.**

If you were driving in the rain, slid off the road, wrapped your car around a tree, and found yourself trapped inside, injured and bleeding, would you want a representative from the department of transportation to say, "I was *against* putting that road through the forest." Or the local school superintendent to say, "I'm *for* spending more money on driver education." Or the auto manufacturer to say, "Our cars have the finest safety records." No, you'd want someone to free you from the wreckage, stop your bleeding, and get you to the hospital!

Too many people today mistake statements for solutions. Lip service is no substitute for *doing* the right thing. Saying you believe in something or that you *intend* to do something doesn't actually accomplish anything positive, yet our culture gives you credit as though it did. But here's the thing: it's totally possible for you to say you are for justice, yet actually oppress people at the same time. You can say you stand for integrity while lying and stealing. You can say anything, but what you *do* shows who you really are. So the next time you see something you believe to be wrong, don't make a statement. Do the right thing. And keep doing it. Eventually, anyone who wants to know what you value or believe will realize your life is your statement.

> **Too many people today mistake statements for solutions.**

5. Stop Placing Blame on Others

About twenty years ago, I became weary and frustrated with the first business organization I founded. I'd started it as a subscription service that sent out monthly lessons on cassette tape to a handful of leaders to help them improve their skills and become more successful. Over time it had grown to offering two lesson-subscription services that reached more than twelve thousand people, hosting multiple large events around the country each year, and creating numerous resources supported not only by the events but also by a call center. Even though I employed a staff of leaders to run the company, it had become so large and demanding that I decided it was time to sell it.

The person who wanted to buy it was the man who then served as the company's president, but he didn't possess the finances needed to make the purchase. Yet he believed he could make one of our events profitable enough to generate the revenue to make the purchase possible. I was unsure of his strategy, because he wanted to engage several very expensive, high-profile speakers to attract a huge audience. But I agreed to it because I wanted to give him a chance to make it work. I knew it was a big risk, but I supported the decision.

The event turned out to be a disaster. It lost $2 million, the company was saddled with a bunch of debt, and the leader who had made the decision left the organization. As a result, I was faced with a decision. What would I do? I could blame him and put the company into bankruptcy. That would be the easiest solution. But I knew failing to pay the debts was not the right thing to do. Besides, as the owner of the company, the buck stopped with me. I was ultimately responsible for the company's decisions, not anyone else.

Margaret and I decided to sell a piece of commercial investment property to pay off the debt. Then we sold the unencumbered company. We lost money. In fact, years later that piece of property sold for three times what we had received for it. But we retained our self-respect because we did what we knew was right. In these kinds of situations, blaming others doesn't solve anything. Neither does letting yourself become resentful or bitter. The right way to move forward is to be pragmatic, forgive, let go, and keep doing the right things for the right reasons.

START PAYING THE PRICE TO STAY ON THE HIGH ROAD

I wish I could tell you that doing the right things for the right reasons doesn't cost anything. But if I did, I wouldn't be telling you the truth. Doing what's right often has a price. That was true when Dad was kind to people who were treating him poorly. It cost him by slowing down his ability to accomplish his goals. It distracted him from the vision. It took a toll on him emotionally and physically. But he continued to travel the high road in the face of those difficult headwinds. As I've explained, I greatly admired that and have striven to imitate him.

As you strive to take the high road by doing what's right for the right reasons, here's what you should expect:

The First Time You Pay Is the Hardest

If doing what's right is a new experience, you will find the first time you pay a price to be the hardest. Why? Because it's new. We expect doing the right thing to be celebrated by all, but it rarely is. The first time I made a tough decision in my leadership, some people didn't like it, and that hurt my feelings because of my desire to please everybody. It made me ask myself, *What's wrong with me? If I were a better leader, would this have happened?* But that was incorrect thinking. Making everyone happy is impossible and shouldn't be anyone's goal as a leader. Doing what's right for the right reasons should be the goal—even if it costs me.

> Doing what's right for the right reasons should be the goal—even if it costs me.

After you've paid a price the first time, the next time will still be hard, but since you've done it before, you'll know you can do it again. Maybe you don't want to, but you can. And each time you pay a price, you gain confidence, self-respect, and awareness that improves your leadership.

You Won't Always Know the Full Cost on the Front End

When I was a young leader, I assumed I would be able to see the costs I would have to pay as a leader to do the right things. I had no idea. For example, in my thirties when I became the leader of Skyline Church in the San Diego area, it was obvious to me that we would eventually need to relocate the church. I understood that on my first visit even before I became the pastor. The building was tired. Our location wasn't good. Our corner had become the turf boundary between three local gangs. Expansion wasn't an option because the property was landlocked. If we grew at all, the only way the church would have a positive future would be to move.

I knew it was the right thing to do. I also knew it would be an uphill battle with a cost. I expected to lose hundreds of people. And I was right about that. However, other costs came up that I didn't anticipate. I badly underestimated the government bureaucracy and regulatory obstructions we would face trying to build in Southern California. We raised money and bought land. We also raised money to build, but we couldn't get the property rezoned. I spent my time communicating the vision to keep it alive and helping my people believe in the dream. But they saw no actual progress being made toward it. I led Skyline for fourteen years, yet when I left, we *still* hadn't even broken ground on the new land. My successor continued the fight, and he was the one who finally built the new facility and relocated the church.

> When people stop growing and improving as leaders, it's seldom due to a lack of capacity or ability. They stop because of an unwillingness to pay the price.

As you do what's right, you are likely to have similar experiences. Some of the costs you will see. Others will be unexpected. In those seasons, if your motives are right and you make the best choice for everyone with the information you have, remind yourself that you're doing what you believe is right.

Your Account Is Never "Paid in Full"

When I've spoken on the topic of paying a price as a leader, many people have come to me and asked, "Well, how often do I have to pay the price? When can I be done?" The answer is *never*. When we're young and inexperienced, we hope and believe we can pay a price once and be done with it. But leadership doesn't work that way. Paying a price is a never-ending process. It's been my observation that when people stop growing and improving as leaders, it's seldom due to a lack of capacity or ability. They stop because of an unwillingness to pay the price. If we want to grow in our leadership and hope to impact a greater number of people on a deeper level on the high road, we need to expect to continue paying.

THE VALUE OF DOING WHAT'S RIGHT OUTWEIGHS THE COSTS

Doing the right thing can cost you time, money, friendships, and opportunities. But what's the cost of *not* doing the right thing? Loss of self-respect. Harm to other people. Guilt. Regret. Damage to your heart and soul. Don't pay that cost. Do the right things and live on the high road. You won't regret it. When you do what's right, you're not only taking the high road with others. You're taking the high road with yourself. You live better and sleep better when your conscience is clear and you've tried to give others your best. On the high road..

> When you do what's right, you're not only taking the high road with others. You're taking the high road with yourself.

> You may lose ground, but you will gain growth.
> You may lose power, but you will gain strength.
> You may lose money, but you will gain wealth.
> You may lose celebrity, but you will gain credibility.

One of the leaders who made these discoveries is Marty Grunder. He owns a landscaping business in Miamisburg, Ohio. He started it as a kid with a twenty-five dollar garage-sale mower because he wanted to make money for college. But what started as a way to make extra money became his profession. After he graduated, he focused his full-time efforts on building a landscape company. He has been running it for more than four decades.

A few years ago, Marty made a mistake in the way he applied fertilizer to the grass of a large number of his clients. It resulted in a lot of damage to their lawns. It was an accident—an honest mistake. There was no denying his company was responsible, but in a situation like that, he could have chosen to do nothing about it, and his clients would not have had an easy time coming after him to pay for the damage.

But Marty was dedicated to doing the right things for the right reasons. Although he knew he would take a big financial hit, he still chose to repair the damage and restore every customer's lawn. It took him several years to recoup his costs, but it was the decision he felt he could live with. He had a clear conscience. And in the long run, he actually benefited financially. The customers whose lawns he had destroyed and then fixed chose to stay with him. And his reputation in his industry and the community rose. As a result, many more people sought out his services. So even though doing the right thing cost him, it ultimately benefited him.

If you want to be a high-road leader, every time you prepare to make a decision or take action, check your motives. Ask yourself why you're doing what you're doing. Whom are you trying to serve? Just yourself? Your team? Your side? Or are you trying to do what's right for everyone? If you try to do the right things for the right reasons every time, you'll always be able to live with yourself, people will trust you, and you'll have an ongoing positive influence with others.

The Pathway to Doing the Right Things for the Right Reasons:
GOOD MOTIVES

To be a high-road leader, you must do the right things for the right reasons. The first question you must ask yourself to know whether your reasons are right is why you want to lead others. Your motives color your leadership more than anything else. They determine whether you will try to take people in a positive direction that will help them or in a negative direction to help you. So, what are your motives? What are your reasons for leading people? Personal gain? Obligation? Duty? Or for the benefit of others? Any answer that doesn't put others first is likely to take you off the high road.

The second question you need to ask is whether you're willing to pay the price of high-road leadership. Doing the right things for the right reasons will always cost a leader, maybe not right away, but eventually it will. You need to be prepared to pay it—and keep paying—if you want to keep leading on the high road. But here's the good news: if you pay the price, once you see the positive results in others' lives, you will find it worth what it costs you.

5

GIVE MORE THAN YOU TAKE

WHAT DOES IT MEAN TO BE A GIVER? HOW DO YOU THINK ABOUT generosity? Many people think those questions have to do with financial wealth. They think about people like Microsoft co-founder Bill Gates and Berkshire-Hathaway chairman and CEO Warren Buffet who famously created the Giving Pledge. In May 2009, they invited a group of fellow billionaires to a dinner gathering in New York City and challenged them to make "a moral commitment to give their fortunes to charity."[44] Buffet and Bill and Melinda Gates were already doing that. They convinced forty US billionaires to sign on that year, and eventually 241 people from 29 countries joined them.[45] But that's not really what generosity is about on the high road.

GIVE OR TAKE

Giving as a high-road leader has nothing to do with wealth. For a high-road leader, the question has nothing to do with how much of your wealth or assets you are giving away. The question is much simpler: Every day of your life, are you *giving* more than you *take*? This applies to every aspect of a high-road leader's life.

In his book *All I Really Need to Know I Learned in Kindergarten*, Robert Fulghum said, "Every person passing through this life will unknowingly leave something and take something away."[46] High-road leaders are givers. They know that every person is a plus or a minus in the lives of other people, and they are determined to be pluses. As a result, they intentionally adopt and maintain a generosity of spirit. Their thinking is different from others'. While most people go through their day wondering what they will receive, high-road leaders are preoccupied with the idea of what they will give. And that's why everyone can become a giver—because it's a mindset. Rich or poor, famous or obscure, young or old, anyone can be someone who gives more than they take.

> Rich or poor, famous or obscure, young or old, anyone can be someone who gives more than they take.

LEARNING TO GIVE

Where does a giving mindset originate? I believe it comes from three kinds of generous thinking:

Open-Hearted Generosity: *I desire to add value to others.*
Open-Minded Generosity: *I think the best of others.*
Open-Handed Generosity: *I give freely and often to others.*

When you value people, think the best of them, and look for ways to give to them, you become the kind of giver who lives on the high road.

Most people have heard the term *good Samaritan*. That's someone who helps a stranger. But maybe you don't know where the phrase originated. The name comes from a parable told in the Bible:

> "A man was going down from Jerusalem to Jericho, when he was attacked by robbers. They stripped him of his clothes, beat him and went away, leaving him half dead. A priest happened to be going down the same road, and when he saw the man, he

passed by on the other side. So too, a Levite, when he came to the place and saw him, passed by on the other side. But a Samaritan, as he traveled, came where the man was; and when he saw him, he took pity on him. He went to him and bandaged his wounds, pouring on oil and wine. Then he put the man on his own donkey, brought him to an inn and took care of him. The next day he took out two denarii and gave them to the innkeeper. 'Look after him,' he said, 'and when I return, I will reimburse you for any extra expense you may have.'"[47]

This story shows three different approaches leaders can have when dealing with other people. The first is displayed by the robbers. They thought, *What's yours is mine!* They were takers and were willing to devalue someone to get what they wanted.

The two religious leaders who passed by the injured man didn't try to take anything from him, but they didn't try to give him anything to help either. They thought, *What's mine is mine.* Their indifference seems almost as cruel as the attitude of the robbers because they also left him for dead.

Only the Samaritan had a giver's mindset—despite the fact that he and the injured Israelite would have been bitter adversaries politically, religiously, and ethnically. The Samaritan thought, *What's mine is yours, and I will give it.* He gave more than he took and was prepared to give even more. He alone of the group acted as a high-road leader.

USE RECEIVING AS INSPIRATION FOR GIVING

When you're in need and a generous giver helps you, it makes a difference in your life. I developed a greater appreciation for generosity when I was in my first job as a leader in Hillham, Indiana. I've already told you about how back then Margaret and I had nothing. At that time, my brother, Larry, and his wife, Anita, were very generous to us. And they still are. When I started my job in Hillham, I owned one black suit. I'd worn it throughout college. If I went to an event, I wore it. If I took Margaret to a dance, I wore it. Every Sunday when I attended church, I wore it. When I preached my first sermon, I wore it. Get the picture?

When I took my new job, I was required to wear a suit while speaking to the same group of people three or more times every week. If it weren't for Larry and Anita, my congregation would have seen me wearing that one suit every time for three years. Larry was already very successful, even though he was only two and a half years older than I was. He took me out and bought me suits and all my other clothes that first year. And the only way Margaret and I were able to take any kind of vacation in those early years was because Larry and Anita took us with them on theirs. No person could ever have a better brother than mine.

> **High-road leadership means living a life that says "I want more *for* you than *from* you."**

There are two ways people often respond to receiving from others. The first is to be glad they were helped and hope they receive help again in the future when they need it. The second is to be grateful and look for opportunities to become givers themselves for the benefit of others.

Over time, Margaret and I learned to give, and the more we gave, the greater the joy we felt. In the second half of our lives, we've been greatly blessed, which to us means we get to give more, and we've set giving goals for ourselves each year. One of the reasons I keep working at my age is that we want to keep giving. The amount of joy we receive from it is almost unfair. I can tell you this: I know plenty of successful people who are unhappy, but I have never met a generous person who was unhappy.

GIVE WHAT YOU CAN

I don't want all this talk about finances to make you think giving more than you take is always about money, because it's not. It's a desire to weight the scales in favor of others. It's a mindset of leaving everyone you meet and every person you lead better off than when you found them. It's the idea of always bringing something to the table for others, but doing so without expecting anything in return. High-road leadership means living a life that says "I want more *for* you than *from* you." When you do that, you've made a high-road decision.

How can you add value to people? What do you have to give that will help others, bless them, show them they matter, and help them get ahead? Everyone on earth has something they can give. The question is whether you will decide to be generous and become intentional about giving. Here are some of the things we can give others as we travel the high road as leaders:

Talent

Every person on the planet has been gifted with talent of some kind, and that talent can be used to serve and add value to others. For example, I know one of my greatest talents is communication. I was born with speaking ability, and I've also worked hard to develop it. How do I give to others using that talent? Every time I am asked to speak, I do everything in my power to exceed expectations. I want every audience member who attends to feel like they got more than their money's worth. I want every host who invites me to communicate to their crowd to feel like I gave more value to them and their people than they paid for.

Similarly, when I write a book, I want people to feel like they received more than they paid for. Yes, I always try to load every book with great content. And I love it when people tell me they read one of my books more than once to get everything out of it. But when someone pays money for a book, I want them to feel like they got something that can change their life. That's worth way more than several dollars.

What are your talents, and how can you use them to give to others? Can you cook? Then you can provide others with great meals. Can you fix things? Then help your neighbors when something breaks down at their house. Are you a good organizer? Volunteer for a nonprofit to help them accomplish their mission with greater efficiency. Can you lead? Then use your skills to not only improve a team but to add value to each individual on it. All you need to do is approach tasks with a heart to serve and the desire to give more than you take.

Time

Each of us gets the same twenty-four hours every day. We all get seven days per week and no more. The only thing we don't know is how many weeks we will get in our lifetime. It's up to us whether we choose to give the time we have to others.

When Warren Buffett signed the Giving Pledge, he said he did so out of gratitude for his extraordinary good fortune. Interestingly, at the same time he noted that he was giving money rather than time. He wrote,

> This pledge does not leave me contributing the most precious asset, which is time. Many people, including—I'm proud to say—my three children, give extensively of their own time and talents to help others. Gifts of this kind often prove far more valuable than money. A struggling child, befriended and nurtured by a caring mentor, receives a gift whose value far exceeds what can be bestowed by a check. My sister, Doris, extends significant person-to-person help daily. I've done little of this.

What I can do, however, is to take a pile of Berkshire Hathaway stock certificates—"claim checks" that when converted to cash can command far-ranging resources—and commit them to benefit others who, through the luck of the draw, have received the short straws in life.[48]

How much time are you willing to give others without asking for anything in return? Can you mentor someone? Can you stop what you're doing to assist someone who's struggling? You never know when a moment will be precious to another person. And you will never find out unless you give it.

Opportunities

As leaders, one of the most important responsibilities we carry is the ability and willingness to give people opportunities. We can help people go places and do things they would never be able to do on their own. Sometimes those opportunities turn out great. Other times they don't. But that's part of being willing to give more than you take.

> You never know when a moment will be precious to another person. And you will never find out unless you are willing to give it.

Marilyn Gist, whom I quoted in chapter 2, writes that the offering of opportunities starts with our awareness of the individual people we lead:

> "Do You See Me?" is perhaps the most critical question people have when asked to work with a leader. It implies: Do I matter to you? Do you understand my view and my needs? Am I merely a pawn for you to use in achieving your goals, or do you care

about me as a person with my own thoughts and needs? Do you get my potential as a partner in this work? And are you willing to work with me even though we will not always see eye to eye?[49]

You won't give to someone you don't see as an individual person, as someone of value. This goes back to the need to value all people if you want to be a high-road leader. It also requires being intentional. Gist suggests that leaders make people feel seen and valued by being treated as partners in their work. This can be done using what Gist calls *generous inclusion*. She explains, "Inclusion means inviting people to be part of the real action."[50] Here's how she suggests that should look:

> **Generosity has everything to do with your mindset, not your net worth.**

GENEROUS INCLUSION

Do	Don't
Encourage people to share ideas and feelings on important issues.	Limit participation to minor discussions and routine matters.
Notice when your power may cause others to defer to you unnecessarily, and encourage them to contribute.	Assume that others have little to offer.
Examine your attitudes toward diversity of all kinds.	Allow biases to result in excluding certain types of people.
Listen deeply—even when others present views that seem unfamiliar or uncomfortable.	Ignore others' views or cut people off when they share opinions.
Present an emotionally welcoming demeanor.	Signal that you are too busy or disinterested to interact with others.[51]

I like the way she explains this. To me, generous inclusion means people don't work *for* me. They work *with* me. And I look for opportunities I can give them to grow, develop, and rise to bigger and better things. If you possess any kind of leader's role, you carry that same responsibility. While people are under your leadership, there are some things they will get to do *only* if you give them the opportunity.

Money

Anyone can be financially generous, whether they possess little or much, because generosity has everything to do with your mindset, not your net worth. That being said, it's a fact that some people have a gift for making money. That's always been true of my brother, Larry. For as long as I remember, he had jobs and worked. When Larry was in high school, my father got him opportunities to work for the best businesspeople in town so that he could learn. He bought his first car for cash when he was sixteen. When Larry went off to college, he saw business opportunities and started investing in real estate while he was taking classes. It's how he had money to give to Margaret and me when he was in only his midtwenties.

When Larry was thirty-nine or forty years old, we were playing tennis and he told me he was thinking of retiring. "I've got all the money Anita and the kids will ever need," he confided.

> **Generous inclusion means people don't work *for* me. They work *with* me.**

We talked it through, and in the end, Larry decided to keep working so that he could have more money to give away. That's what he's done for the last forty years. He is still one of the most generous people I know.

You don't need to be wealthy to use money to add value to people. You can do it in little ways. I can't think of anything that brings me greater joy than being generous. One of my favorite things to do is give generous tips to servers, hotel workers, valets, and groundskeepers working on a golf course. I'll often tell them what a good job they're doing. Sometimes when I give someone an unexpected tip, like a groundskeeper, I'll let them know I'm doing it because God loves and values them. It's important to remember that what you give to someone may not be big to you, but it may be huge to them. And that's the point.

Connections

For years I've talked about how I schedule lunches with people who are better leaders or more successful than I am so that I can ask questions and learn from them. I've explained these "learning lunches" before in my books. One of the questions I always ask at each lunch is, "Who do you know that I should know?" Their answers to that question have led to more great connections with other people than I could possibly count.

What I haven't talked about before is how I turn that question around for the benefit of others. When I meet someone and get to know them, I think to myself, *Who do I know that they should know?* Then I find ways to connect them.

Experiences

One of the best things you can do as a leader is give others experiences, especially if those experiences are something they cannot do for themselves. I do this intentionally all the time. I look ahead at my calendar and think through how I can include people in my own experiences or create new ones. Sometimes it means taking an employee with me. When I went on my first book tour for *The 21 Irrefutable Laws of Leadership*, I took my writing partner, Charlie Wetzel, with me on the private jet leased by my publisher so that we could experience that together. When my company plans an event like Exchange, which we describe as a leadership experience, we plan something they will always remember. One year we went to the New York Stock Exchange after-hours so participants could enjoy drinks and appetizers on the floor of the Exchange, eat dinner in the boardroom, and have their photos taken ringing the bell. Another year we took a private tour of the Churchill War Rooms in London, where they also got to meet and ask questions of Sir Nicholas Soames, Winston Churchill's grandson.

I don't do this only in my professional life. I also do it with my family. On their birthdays, each of my five grandchildren know an original poem written by their papa will be waiting for them when they wake up. One Christmas I encouraged the members of Margaret's family, who are not naturally demonstrative, to share what they love and value about one another. To this day, they talk about that as one of their favorite Christmas memories.

I also look for opportunities to create experiences daily. I review my schedule every morning and I think about who I'll be spending time with and what we will be doing. And I intentionally think of ways I can create experiences for people that are personal and meaningful. It may be as simple as signing a book and giving it to them or inviting people to the table for a special dinner and facilitating a great discussion by asking questions. All it takes is thinking ahead, thinking about the person, and doing something that makes them feel special and appreciated. Do that, and you will distinguish yourself as a leader.

YOU CAN'T GIVE WHAT YOU DON'T HAVE

In the end, we are stewards of whatever we have in life. It's up to us to use what we have access to for the benefit of others. Bill and Melinda Gates recognized this and it motivated them to use their wealth for greater purposes than their own enjoyment, including co-creating the

Giving Pledge. They said, "Both of us were fortunate to grow up with parents who taught us some tremendously important values.... And if life happens to bless you with talent or treasure, you have a responsibility to use those gifts as well and as wisely as you possibly can.... We feel very lucky to have the chance to work together in giving back the resources we are stewards of."[52]

Perhaps the most important truth about being able to give more than you take on the high road is that to be a giver, you must have something to give. If you want to give money, you need to earn it by working, investing, or building a business. If you want to give anything else, you must develop it through personal growth. And if you want to *continue* giving, you must commit yourself to growing throughout your lifetime.

My realization about the importance of growth came to me over time, starting in my twenties. It proceeded like this:

1. I Needed to Grow

The process started with awareness that I needed to become intentional about growing or I would not improve personally or professionally. Like many people, I thought experience alone would make me better. But I realized that without a plan, I might work harder, but I might never work smarter. That's when I bought my first personal growth kit. It was a curriculum that taught me how to prioritize, set goals, and work toward them.

2. I Needed to Target My Growth

After spending two years working through that initial program, I got a taste for growth. I loved improving myself and I began to see the results of it in my performance. So I started looking around for other resources that would help me. I'd always been a reader, but I became more targeted in my reading, choosing books that I believed would help me. I began reading books every month to improve myself.

I also began to study what made people successful. I observed and interviewed good leaders. I read more broadly. As a result I discovered that successful people excelled in four areas: relationships, equipping, attitude, and leadership. So that's where I began to focus my growth with high intentionality.

3. I Needed to Apply and Practice What I've Been Learning

The more I learned, the more I put what I knew into practice. And the more I put what I knew into practice, the more successful I became. My life and my career started to gain momentum.

4. I Needed to Share What I've Been Learning to Help Others

As I gained success, others began asking me for advice. That's when I began sharing the insights I'd gained from my personal growth journey. I started teaching How to Be a R.E.A.L. Success—through relationships, equipping, attitude, and leadership. The more I taught, the more people wanted to know, and the more I knew I needed to keep growing so that I could continue giving what I had.

5. I Need to Continue Growing for the Sake of Others

Today I keep climbing and growing for the sake of others. I'm no longer motivated by success. I'm motivated by significance, which can come to fruition only through giving. It's another reason I stay in the game in my late seventies. The more I earn and the more I learn, the more I have to return to others. My hope is to keep giving until I'm empty. And I don't believe that will happen anytime soon.

That is also my hope for you. I hope you use your time, your talents, and your opportunities to give to others. I hope you'll approach every day asking yourself, *What can I give today? How can I add value to the people who work with me? How can I help others to grow and get better? Whose day can I make better just by being there and giving more than I take?*

> **The more I earn and the more I learn, the more I have to return to others.**

Everyone has something to give, so don't wait to start giving more than you take. Start today. Be a river, not a reservoir. High-road leaders aren't hoarders. Start earning and learning to make yourself more valuable to others so you can start returning. And embrace a spirit of generosity. You'll never regret it.

The Pathway to Giving More Than You Take:
AN ABUNDANCE MINDSET

The greatest obstacle most people face on the pathway to giving more than they take is a scarcity mindset. Too many people worry that there's not enough to go around. As a result, they hoard whatever they have. They believe giving freely will leave them without. What they don't understand is that giving is one of the most powerful and rewarding things they can do, not just for others, but for themselves. When you possess a scarcity mindset, you hold tight to what you have, fearing you will lose it. Ironically, because your hand is closed, you can't receive more. The way to overcome this obstacle is to embrace the idea of abundance. If you give, your hand opens, and it is in position to receive more.

The history of humanity is literally a history of abundance. When there weren't enough trained scribes to copy books, the printing press was invented, and today billions of books are available to read. When people felt limited by what they could do with their own hands or the power of horses, they discovered how to harness electricity and the power of steam. When one natural resource seems in danger of running out, others are discovered, such as nuclear power and solar energy.

Possess an abundance mindset and a giver's spirit, and you will want to give more than you take in every situation. Give generously and you will never be the same again. Neither will the people you lead.

6

DEVELOP EMOTIONAL CAPACITY

IF YOU'VE BEEN A LEADER FOR ANY LENGTH OF TIME, I'M SURE YOU'VE noticed that leading people today is difficult. I've been leading for more than half a century, and it's never been tougher. As I write this, the setbacks and fallout of the COVID pandemic of 2020 and 2021 continue to challenge us. People are struggling emotionally. They're fragile, and they often engage in dysfunctional behavior, which means their thinking and actions are, by definition, "characterized by abnormal or unhealthy interpersonal behavior or interaction."[53] According to the National Alliance on Mental Illness, depression is the leading cause of disability worldwide. This and anxiety disorders cost the global economy $1 trillion each year. In the United States, more than a fourth of all adults experience anxiety disorders or major depressive episodes.[54]

In an environment such as this, many people want to opt out. They want to shelter in place, as they did during COVID, and disengage from the challenges of life. But leaders can't do that. If you are a leader, people are relying on you to help them and improve their situations. As leaders, we must weather the storms, make hard decisions, and lead people to a better place.

Since leadership is such a high-pressure job, we need to possess a high level of emotional capacity. If we're drowning, we can't save other people who are drowning. If we're locked up emotionally, we will find it difficult or impossible to take the high road because leadership requires high emotional capacity.

HOW TO INCREASE YOUR EMOTIONAL CAPACITY

When I say *emotional capacity*, what do I mean? I'm talking about the ability to respond to adversity, failure, criticism, and pressure in positive ways. Strong leaders who travel the high road are able to stand up under the pressure of internal conflict, adverse situations, and difficult people. They demonstrate resilience and emotional strength in difficult times. They lead themselves well and manage their emotions so that they can lead others well. And the good news is that it is possible to make choices that reduce unneeded stress, develop emotional capacity, and increase the ability to work under pressure. Here are eight ways to do that:

1. Refuse to See Yourself as a Victim

One of the most damaging things we can do to undermine our emotional capacity is to see ourselves as victims and feel sorry for ourselves. It disempowers us. If we believe everyone else is responsible for where we are in life or that the world owes us something, we put ourselves at a great disadvantage. As Mark Twain said, "Don't go around saying the world owes you a living; the world owes you nothing; it was here first."[55]

Psychologist and author Arlin Cuncic described the characteristics of people with a victim mentality. She said they believe:

- Bad things have happened in the past and will continue to happen to them.
- Others are to blame for their misfortune.
- There is no point in trying to make a change because it will not work.[56]

Robert E. Quinn, author of *Deep Change*, goes even further. He described people who see themselves as victims as being like the walking dead:

> When people join legions of the walking dead, they begin to live lives of "quiet desperation." They tend to experience feelings of meaninglessness, hopelessness, and impotence in their work roles, often taking on the role of "poor victim." A victim is a person who suffers a loss because of the actions of others. A victim tends to believe that salvation comes only from the actions of others. They have little choice but to whine and wait until something good happens. Living with someone who chooses to play the victim role is draining; working in an organization where many people have chosen the victim role is absolutely depressing. Like a disease, the condition tends to spread.[57]

Possessing a victim mindset is personally discouraging, emotionally draining, and relationally destructive. Furthermore, it makes good leadership nearly impossible, because no one can be a victim and lead effectively at the same time.

If you have a tendency to see yourself as a victim and feel sorry for yourself, how can you combat it?

Take Responsibility for Your Life

The first and most important step is to take ownership for your life and your choices. My parents instilled this sense of personal responsibility into me and my siblings when we were young, and I have made it a priority to keep living out that value into adulthood and instill it in my own children and grandchildren. I focus on taking responsibility in several areas, with these being the most important to me:

- Attitude—I recognize that my attitude is a choice and I work at keeping it positive every day.
- Time—I acknowledge I have only a set number of hours in a day, and I control how I use them. I don't allow others to dictate my schedule.
- Priorities—I identify and work to act on the most important things every day and do my best not to allow lesser things to distract me.
- Potential—I am responsible for my own personal growth and maximizing my God-given potential; if I don't develop it, no one else will.
- Passion—I don't wait for others to inspire and motivate me; I fuel and fan the spark that's in me and look forward to getting up every morning.
- Calling—I am responsible for the gifts and opportunities God gives me, and I work to make the most of them to do what I was put on earth to do.

> **There are never two consecutive good days in any leader's life.**

Knowing that there are certain facts of life that you *can't* control, do you take active responsibility for your life and every choice you *can* make? If you haven't in the past, start doing so now. It's an important step toward developing emotional capacity.

Don't Build Your Life Around Your Troubles

One day I was reading an article about problems some leaders in my profession were having, and I remarked to Margaret, "Why do these leaders have so many problems when I don't?" She just laughed.

"What?" I asked.

Don't you think you have a lot of problems too?"

I started to think about it, and I soon realized she was right. I did deal with problems all the time. As the saying goes, there are never two consecutive good days in any leader's life. Leadership is problem-solving. And that's when it hit me: while I have my share of problems, I don't let them hold me back. My focus is on solutions and moving forward, and I don't let my problems define or stop me. Focus your life upon your opportunities, not your problems. Focus on the vision you want to accomplish, not the obstacles along the way.

> It's always more effective to act your way into feeling than to feel your way into action.

Make Action Your Priority

Do you have issues you could address but instead have accepted and become comfortable with? If so, these issues may be draining your emotional energy, keeping you from leading effectively, and blocking you from reaching your potential. Don't allow that. Instead, take action to resolve them. Don't rationalize or defend why you must live with these issues. Don't complain about what you permit. Instead, do something about it.

Psychologist George W. Crane said, "Remember, motions are the precursors of emotions. You can't control the latter directly but only through your choice of motions or actions."[58] He made this remark in the context of couples resolving marital difficulties and overcoming misunderstandings, but the principle applies more broadly to any kind of difficulty. It's always more effective to act your way into feeling than to feel your way into action.

Around the time I graduated from college, I read a book by Og Mandino titled *The Greatest Salesman in the World*, a kind of parable about maintaining a positive attitude. In it was a poem that stayed with me. Mandino wrote:

> If I feel depressed I will sing.
> If I feel sad I will laugh.
> If I feel ill I will double my labor.
> If I feel fear I will plunge ahead....
> If I feel poverty I will think of wealth to come.
> If I feel incompetent I will remember past success.
> If I feel insignificant I will remember my goals....
> Today I will be the master of my emotions.[59]

As you can see, the key to dealing positively with negative emotions is to take action. Whenever you feel stuck, if you can do something positive, it will help you.

Express Gratitude

The final way to prevent yourself from feeling like a victim is to express gratitude. I love a story I read several years ago about acting icon Charlton Heston, star of epic films like *Ben-Hur* and *The Ten Commandments*. In 2002, Heston disclosed that he had been diagnosed with Alzheimer's. Not long after that, he was with his close friend and publicist Tony Makris. Heston noticed his friend was down and asked, "Why so glum, pal—you feel bad for me?" When Makris nodded, Heston responded, "Don't. I got to be Charlton Heston for almost eighty years. That's more than fair."[60]

If developing gratitude is difficult for you, follow the advice of psychiatrist Judith Orloff:

> The way I snap out of victim mentality is by remembering how blessed my life is compared with much of our global family. I'm not fighting to survive genocide, poverty, or daily street violence from an insurgency militia. I have the luxury to feel

lonely when I'm without a romantic partner or get irked by an annoying person. I have the gift of time to surmount negative emotions. Seeing things this way stops me from wallowing, an imprisoning indulgence. So, when you think you're having a bad day, try to keep this kind of perspective.[61]

The bottom line is that if you see yourself as a victim, you give your power away. You won't be an advocate for yourself. You won't work to solve problems. You will be more likely to become fatalistic. You will be less likely to try to help others. And you will become emotionally exhausted. None of that will help you to develop greater emotional capacity. Only by taking responsibility for yourself will you remain positive and proactive, which makes you better able to live and lead on the high road.

> **The bottom line is that if you see yourself as a victim, you give your power away.**

2. Control Your Emotions and Process Them Quickly

To work well with people and make good decisions, which are at the heart of high-road leadership, you can't let your emotions overwhelm you. Maybe you find it easy to control your emotions under pressure. But what if you're a highly emotional person who has a difficult time keeping strong emotions in check? What can you do to improve your ability? I recommend you try something that author, speaker, and financial coach Toyin Crandell teaches her clients. She coaches them to identify their "emotional homes." This is designed to ground them when negative emotions threaten to overwhelm them. She has observed that leaders with strong emotions sometimes make poor decisions when pressure builds. She coaches leaders to identify the three negative emotions that most often cloud their judgment, and for each they must then identify an opposing positive emotion they can tap into to counteract it and get to a better place.

For example, if a person is prone to sadness under pressure, she recommends they make *gratitude* an emotional home and practice tapping into it when they're feeling sad. She chose gratitude because it is easier to tap into than trying to be happy, yet it still leads there. If someone is easily frustrated, she recommends they tap into *resourcefulness* to counter it.

In emotional situations, Crandell said, "People get stuck in an unproductive state because their brains are no longer thinking logically and clearly enough to know where to go. They want out [of that state], but they can't find the door. Knowing your emotional home gives you a clear road map to the door so you can step out of the pressure and into the sunlight. There they can see clearly again and make decisions that move their business, team, or organization forward despite the pressure."

> "Psychologists have discovered that 95 percent of your emotions are determined by the way you talk to yourself as you go through your day." – Brian Tracy

Crandell points out that this isn't a way to suppress emotions but rather to process them. "Having an emotional home doesn't mean you ignore your natural human responses. They are a healthy part of our human experience," she observed. "It simply helps you learn how to fully feel and process the emotion that was triggered *without making a poor decision*, and then redirect your heart to your chosen positive emotional state."[62]

I process my emotions pretty quickly, but I still take time to reflect, not only to make sure my mind and heart are clear after conflict or a high-pressure situation, but also to make sure I learn from it. I believe an event isn't over until I've learned from it. To reflect, I do the following:

- **Review My Day by Myself.** Every evening I take a break and spend time alone thinking about the previous twenty-four hours by asking myself the question, *What happened in my world today?*
- **Think About Myself.** We don't learn anything unless we take time to reflect. To evaluate my experiences of the day, I ask, *What did I learn about myself today?*
- **Talk to Myself.** What you do with your observations and what you say to yourself about them has a huge impact on you. Speaker Brian Tracy said, "Psychologists have discovered that 95 percent of your emotions are determined by the way you talk to yourself as you go through your day."[63] To help this process, I ask, *What do I need to hear myself say?*
- **Direct Myself.** Reflection has great value for learning, but much of that is lost if we don't decide what we should *do* with what we've learned. So I ask, *How should I apply what I've learned?*
- **Take Action Myself.** Time reflecting and processing emotions is wasted if it does not ultimately lead to positive action. What's more, positive action leads to positive emotions. That's why I ask myself, *Will I follow through with action?*

Every time you process negative emotions, redirect yourself to positive emotions, learn from the situation, and act on what you've learned, you take a positive big step toward increasing your emotional capacity.

3. Keep Short Accounts

One of the best things you can do to increase your emotional capacity is to process conflict quickly and keep yourself from carrying emotional baggage or keeping score. I'll explain more about these ideas in subsequent chapters, but I'll say this now: I refuse to carry around negative emotions toward other people. I love what actor and comedian Buddy Hackett said when he was asked about conflict. He responded, "I've had a few arguments with people, but I never carry a grudge. You know why? While you're carrying a grudge, they're out dancing."[64]

Anger, resentment, jealousy, envy, bitterness, grudges—these things weigh us down. Meanwhile, the target of our negative emotions is usually unaffected. The best way to live is to resolve any conflict as quickly as possible. If I'm in the wrong, I apologize immediately and try to make amends. If the other person is in the wrong, I make the intentional choice to forgive them. And then I move on. I have places to go and important tasks to accomplish. It would slow me down and hinder my leadership if I allowed myself to get bogged down by negative emotions. As Elbert Hubbard observed,

> A retentive memory may be a good thing but the ability to forget is the true token of greatness. Successful people forget. They know the past is irrevocable. They're running a race. They can't afford to look behind. Their eye is on the finish line. Magnanimous people forget. They're too big to let little things disturb them. They forget easily. If anyone does them wrong, they consider the source and keep cool. It's only the small people who cherish revenge. Be a good forgetter. Business dictates it, and success demands it.[65]

You won't get very far on the high road as a leader if your focus is on the rearview mirror. You must look ahead and concentrate on the tasks at hand. Alvin Dark, former manager of the Kansas City Athletics and other major-league teams, said, "There's no such thing as taking a pitcher out. There's only bringing another pitcher in."[66] He meant that when you're in the middle of trying to win the game, you don't waste time looking back at the problems created in the earlier innings. You focus on getting the next batter out. Only after the last out of the last inning when the game is over does it make any sense to look back at your mistakes. And even then, the goal should be to learn from them, not carry a grudge.

4. Put Other People's Opinions in Perspective

One of the most limiting beliefs people hold is that others' opinions about them are more important than their own. German poet Friedrich Klopstock remarked, "He who has no opinion of his own, but depends on the opinions of others is a slave."[67] I didn't understand this idea when I was young. I was overly concerned with the opinions of others and let what other people thought hold me back.

> **One of the most limiting beliefs people hold is that others' opinions about them are more important than their own.**

When I started my career, I was leading a church where the congregation voted every year on whether they would retain their leader. At the completion of my first year, they took the required vote, and the results were thirty-one yeses, one no, and one abstention. I was devastated. I had expected the vote to be unanimous. Since it wasn't, I wondered if I should resign. When I called Dad to get his advice about it, he laughed and said, "Stay. It's probably the best vote you'll ever get."

I chose to stay, but I couldn't let it go emotionally. Every Sunday, I looked at the seventy people sitting before me and wondered, *Who voted against me?* One of the people I was teaching didn't like me. Well, two actually, because an abstention is really a *no* without courage.

> "Do not be too concerned about what others may think of you. Be very concerned about what you think of yourself." – *John Wooden*

For six months I engaged in this petty and foolish thinking. Then something happened. I realized I had only a certain amount of energy, and to lead effectively, I needed the energy I had to be positive, not negative. I wanted to expend my energy on what was important. I asked myself, *How many days of my life am I going to keep asking this stupid question?* I realized what a dumb thing I was doing, and I determined to stop being a people pleaser and start being a principled leader. To do that, I took specific steps:

- **I placed my values ahead of the people I wanted to please.** To be faithful to myself and my leadership vision, I had to stop trying to make everyone happy, especially when the people who criticized the most always contributed the least to the organization's success.
- **I thought more about looking forward than looking backward.** I was determined to reach for my potential. That meant focusing on tomorrow more than yesterday. If my old friends wanted to live in the past or settle, I would keep moving forward even if they wouldn't join me.
- **I found new models to emulate.** I began to read books, go to conferences, and seek mentors who would challenge me to stretch. This helped me put more emphasis on growth regardless of what other people thought of me.
- **I moved away from people who were holding me back.** It's very difficult for a people pleaser to reject anyone or be rejected by them. But to grow, I had to be willing to do that.

Anytime I sensed people were trying to manipulate me or make me feel guilty for not doing what they wanted, I let them know I was not going to be swayed from what I believed was important, and I distanced myself from them.

This took me some time, but eventually I was able to follow the advice of coach John Wooden: "Do not be too concerned about what others may think of you. Be very concerned about what you think of yourself."[68]

To be a good leader, you need positive energy. When you don't put other people's opinions in perspective, you end up expending your energy in a nonproductive way. When someone criticizes you or expresses negative opinions about you, if you're in the wrong, then it's your concern and you need to work on yourself to fix it. But if the criticism or negative comments are not true, you shouldn't take them to heart. Don't let someone else's issue become yours. The best thing you can do as a high-road leader is not to take the bait. The moment you let yourself be sucked in emotionally, you're playing their negative game, and that game is not worthy of your time and attention. As author, teacher, and speaker Leo Buscaglia said, "The easiest thing to be in the world is you. The most difficult thing to be is what other people want you to be. Don't let them put you in that position."[69]

> "The easiest thing to be in the world is you. The most difficult thing to be is what other people want you to be. Don't let them put you in that position." – Leo Buscaglia

5. Understand the Difference Between a Problem and a Fact of Life

The fastest way to increase your emotional capacity and reduce your stress is to keep yourself from getting caught up in issues you cannot control or which aren't your concern. I learned this lesson from Fred Smith Sr., a longtime mentor, when I was in my thirties. He and I were having breakfast one morning, and I was complaining about a problem that was annoying me. He didn't let me go on for very long before he stopped me.

"John," he said, "what you're complaining about isn't a problem."

"It's not?" I responded. Hadn't he been listening?

"No. It's a fact of life. You need to know the difference."

Fred went on to explain that for something to be labeled a problem, it has to be solvable. You must be able to *do* something about it. In contrast, a fact of life cannot be changed, so expending time, mental energy, or effort on it is wasted. Complaining about a fact of life is like howling at the moon. Here are some examples of facts of life you cannot change or control:

- Where you were born
- Your genes
- What you did yesterday
- What other people say or do
- The weather
- The stock market
- Death

These are things we need to accept because we cannot change or solve them.

One of the greatest causes of frustration and wastes of physical and emotional energy is worrying about something you can do nothing about. So many people make issues of things that shouldn't be issues, things that are inconsequential or unchangeable. They dwell on them. They ruminate over them. They allow them to create a lot of negative energy in their lives. As an issue bogs them down, they lose sight of the big picture. All of us can fall into that trap. When we do, it holds us back. It keeps us from going where we need to go and doing what we want to do. We need to let go of those things, focus on where we can make a positive difference, and direct our energy accordingly. That's part of choosing to take the high road as a leader.

6. Become Comfortable with Discomfort

Developing emotional capacity does not mean always playing it safe or staying in your comfort zone. That's avoidance. All progress requires change. Great progress involves risk. Those are usually uncomfortable. How should you deal with this? By focusing on your vision and tapping into your desire to reach it. When your sense of purpose is greater than your sense of fear, you are able to master your emotions enough to move forward. No wonder professor Betty Bender said, "Anything I've ever done that ultimately was worthwhile ... initially scared me to death."[70]

My friend Greg Smith, a businessperson and lifelong martial artist, told me something that Sifu Ted Wong, a top student of Bruce Lee, used to ask his students: "What is the process of walking?" Inevitably, a student would say, "Putting your foot out in front of you."

"No," Sifu Wong would say. "If you only put your foot in front of you, you do not move. In order to move, you must throw yourself off balance; your foot just catches your fall."[71]

> "Anything I've ever done that ultimately was worthwhile ... initially scared me to death." – Betty Bender

Being off-balance isn't comfortable. When we take our first steps as children, we are fearful. We worry about falling down, and we *do* fall down. But over time, we learn to become comfortable with our discomfort. As leaders, we need to adopt that same mindset so that we don't get overwhelmed emotionally. We need to embrace risk. Being outside our comfort zone must become normal. Otherwise, we grow complacent, which is like a slow death to a leader. NBA champion coach and Miami Heat president Pat Riley said, "Complacency is the last hurdle any winner, any team must overcome before attaining potential greatness. Complacency is the Success Disease; it takes root when you're feeling good about who you are and what you have achieved."[72]

7. Keep Growing Your Capacity So It's Always Greater Than Your Responsibilities

One of the greatest causes of stress for leaders is having their responsibilities outweigh their capacity to fulfill them with excellence. Any significant gap between what we are capable of doing and what we are required to do puts us in a place of great tension and drains our mental, physical, and emotional energy. Here's how this typically looks:

> When Responsibilities > Capacity: We Experience Burnout
> When Responsibilities = Capacity: We Experience Chronic Stress
> When Responsibilities < Capacity: We Experience Sustainable Success

To maintain good emotional capacity as leaders, we must either manage our responsibilities better or gain greater capacity. This is vital if we want to sustain success as leaders, especially if we want to lead on the high road. Here are my recommendations for how to adjust your level of responsibilities and grow in capacity:

Find Healthy Ways to Manage Your Responsibilities

If you are in the habit of taking on more responsibilities than you can handle, you need to **establish better boundaries.** You can do that by identifying others' expectations for you and making sure they align with your capabilities. If they don't, you'll need to redefine, reclarify, or renegotiate the expectations. Maybe something you thought was essential isn't. Maybe something you believed was an obligation is actually an option. Maybe what was expected of you wasn't realistic and needs to be rethought. One thing is certain: if you don't make adjustments, you will continue to feel stressed and drain your emotional capacity.

Another way to manage your responsibilities is to **count the cost of your commitments**. Every commitment we make comes with a price tag. Calculating the price before making a promise protects us from overextending ourselves. If you've already made a commitment you didn't weigh before you agreed to it and you've discovered you can't keep it, you will need to revisit it and admit your mistake.

A third way to manage your responsibilities in a healthy way is to **align them with your purpose**. Without a clear and compelling picture of your destination in life, you'll waste time and energy on tasks that don't matter. That can definitely drain your energy and discourage you.

Seek Proactive Ways to Increase Your Capacity

Many people I've encountered believe their capacity is set, but that simply isn't true. You can increase your capacity in nearly any area of your life. I believe in this idea so much that I wrote an entire book about it called *No Limits*. Don't allow anyone—yourself included—to tell you that you can't grow, improve, and increase your capacity. If you believe you can increase your emotional capacity and work at it, then you can. If you're convinced you can't, you won't.

To start the process, **focus on your strengths**. When most of us were kids, we were told to spend our time working to pull up our lowest grade. Our teachers wanted us to focus on improving in our areas of weakness. This may be good advice for improving a grade point average, but it's bad advice for reaching your potential. Where you are strongest, you have the greatest potential to grow. At first, your increases in capacity will take large leaps. Later the progress slows down, but if you maintain a long-term mindset about it, you will keep growing. I'm in my late seventies, and I'm still increasing my leadership capacity. My intention is to keep doing that as long as I live.

Another way to increase your emotional capacity is to **manage your energy every day.** If you're proactive in focusing on your priorities and working at the time of day when you're sharp and energized, you will accomplish a lot *and* feel good about yourself doing it, which gives you greater mental and emotional margin. I like to think of every day as having seasons.

> "Nothing builds self-esteem and self-confidence like accomplishment."
> – Thomas Carlyle

For me, early morning is like the spring. I'm fresh and energized. Ideas grow and bloom like flowers. I love to get up before sunrise to write and think. That's when I'm most productive. Afternoon is like autumn. There's a coziness to it. That's when I prefer to spend time with people. I'll attend meetings, make phone calls, or sit and chat. Evenings are like summer. In the hot months, farmers work their land. In the evening, I work on business. And during the nighttime? I rest.

Know yourself and when you're at your best, focus on your priorities, and work in your strengths, and you'll increase your work capacity. As Thomas Carlyle said, "Nothing builds self-esteem and self-confidence like accomplishment."[73] And the better you feel about yourself, the more energy and emotional capacity you'll have to deal with everything else.

8. Make Caring for Yourself a Priority

One of the best things you can do to increase your emotional capacity is take care of yourself. Writer and activist Parker Palmer said, "Self-care is never a selfish act—it is simply good stewardship of the only gift I have, the gift I was put on earth to offer others. Anytime we can listen to true self and give the care it requires, we do it not only for ourselves, but for the many others whose lives we touch."[74]

For the sake of the people we lead, we must take care of ourselves. A rested and recharged leader is more capable of taking the high road when pressure comes and the demands of leadership are high. And that requires more than simply surfing the web or watching mindless TV after work. We must be intentional about rebuilding our energy reserves to re-create ourselves, which means being refreshed and restored.

To be at my best, I focus on caring for myself in four areas.

Seeking Spiritual Nourishment

For me, everything begins with acknowledging a greater source in my life. That not only encourages me and gives me a place to turn when I face challenges, but it also humbles me. Every day I ask God for guidance.

Receiving Relational Energy

Two things give me relational energy. The first is spending time with people I love. I am energized being with Margaret, our kids, and our grandchildren. I also enjoy being with my team members and other leaders. Nothing's more fun than great conversation over a fantastic meal. The second is investing time in people who value growth. I'm energized not only by helping them, but also by seeing them succeed.

Maintaining Physical Health

You might not guess it from looking at me, but I do work on my physical health. I'm rarely sick. I make it my goal to swim for thirty minutes every day. And I work at eating better, though I admit that is my greatest struggle. I want to stay in the game as long as I can.

Promoting Mental Growth

Every day I fill my mind with good thoughts and ideas. I know the only guarantee for a better tomorrow is personal growth today. For that reason, every day I read. I think and ask questions. I file what I'm learning. And I write. I intend to keep learning and growing until I die.

The essence of high-road leadership is serving people and giving your best to them. That's possible only if you have something to give and you possess the capacity to give it. The less emotional baggage you carry, the further you will be able to go. The more you focus on what really matters and let other things go, the less distracted you will be from your greater purpose. The more you work on your emotional capacity, the more margin you will have and the more resilient you will be. All of these things will put you in a better place to lead for the sake of others, no matter what life throws at you.

> **The essence of high-road leadership is serving people and giving your best to them. That's possible only if you have something to give and you possess the capacity to give it.**

The Pathway to Developing Emotional Capacity:
RESILIENCE

The key to developing greater emotional capacity is resilience, which is the "ability to recover from or adjust easily to misfortune or change."[75] Strong leaders are willing to bear the emotional brunt of problems, challenges, setbacks, and other difficulties for the sake of their people and organization. They learn to rebound quickly and help others to bounce back. And because they have created emotional capacity for themselves, they are able to rally their people, challenge and inspire them forward, and navigate them to success.

7

PLACE PEOPLE ABOVE YOUR OWN AGENDA

IN 2016, I WAS APPROACHED BY A WELL-FUNDED POLITICAL GROUP that was frustrated by the state of American politics. Like many people in the United States at the time, they were disillusioned with both political parties and their activities. They especially lacked confidence in the two nominees the parties put forward to run for president: Hillary Clinton and Donald Trump. When I met with representatives of this group, they had a proposal for me to consider. They wanted me to run for president as a third-party candidate.

At first, I was shocked. While I love leadership, study American presidents, and participate in the system by voting, I've never had political aspirations. Not once in my life had it occurred to me to run for office—any office. But I was intrigued. Like many people, I was frustrated with partisan politics, the games, the infighting, and the inability of Washington, DC, to get anything important accomplished. So I gave the idea serious consideration.

I took about two weeks to weigh the idea from every angle. I talked to leaders I respected to get their advice. I spoke to every member of my family because when a person runs for office, everyone in their family is affected. In the end, I declined their offer. First, I believed I could not win the race. No third-party candidate has ever won a presidential election, not even the popular Theodore Roosevelt. It was also late in the game to start a run for office. I concluded I could be nothing better than a spoiler, like Ross Perot in 1992. He received 19 percent of the popular vote while only 6 percent separated winner Bill Clinton from incumbent George H. W. Bush.[76] Many people believed the majority of those voters came from Bush's column.[77]

But there was a second reason I decided not to run. When the third-party representatives discussed the possibility of my running, they said, "Now you need to understand, within twenty-four hours of declaring your candidacy, they will do everything they can to discredit you. People will start telling lies about you. They will tell lies about your family. They'll know what they're saying isn't true, but all they have to do is lie for three months, then the election will be over."

Sadly, I could see this happening to me. Some people in the two political parties will do almost anything to win. And later when I talked with my friend Carly Fiorina, who ran to become the Republican nominee in 2016, she basically said that she had thought the boardrooms of Fortune 100 companies were rough until she ran for political office. In the business community, it's difficult to continually lie and get away with it. In politics, people do.

WHAT'S YOUR AGENDA?

Good leaders get things done. Warren Bennis, one of my favorite leadership writers and thinkers, said, "Leadership is the capacity to translate a vision into reality." Leaders have a bias toward action so they can accomplish things. They like mobilizing people and putting them in motion to see their vision come to fruition. Sometimes leaders possess a goal they want to see accomplished. Other times it's a cause they want to champion. Or there is an issue they want to tackle or a problem they want to solve. Or they want their side to win. In other words, leaders always have an agenda.

PLACE PEOPLE ABOVE YOUR OWN AGENDA

That can be a great thing. But it can also be terrible if the leaders place their agenda ahead of people. At what point does an agenda, a vision, or a cause become more important than people? My answer is *never*. People are always of the highest value. Low-road leaders put others "in their place" by elevating themselves above everyone else. High-road leaders know the right "place" for others is above them.

> **How we see people is how we treat people.**

That's why Jesus, whom I consider to be the greatest high-road leader of all, measured greatness by how people put others ahead of themselves and served them.[78]

How we see people is how we treat people. As I work to accomplish a vision, the way I interact with others will be determined by my perspective:

> If I see you as *hurting*, I'll want to *help* you.
> If I see you as *broken*, I'll want to *fix* you.
> If I see you as *inconvenient*, I'll want to *ignore* you.
> If I see you as an *obstacle*, I'll want to *remove* you.
> If I see you as *competition*, I'll want to *defeat* you.
> But if I see you as *valuable*, I'll want to *serve* you.

If I see you as anything less than valuable, I won't serve you. And if I won't serve you, I'll put my agenda ahead of your best interests.

High-road leaders are willing to serve others. They understand that nothing they want to accomplish is possible unless the people they lead are successful. They know they can't accomplish anything worthwhile alone. They understand that they need the people, and the people need them.

HOW TO PLACE PEOPLE FIRST

If you're a highly driven and productive leader, does placing people first mean you have to give up trying to accomplish your vision? No, of course not. It simply means considering others and their interests first. Here are four simple things you can do to grow in this area:

1. Develop Empathy Intentionally

Willingness to place people above your own agenda begins with empathy. We must listen to others and work to understand them better. We must imagine ourselves walking in their shoes and attempt to see things from their point of view. This can be difficult, especially if we are used to listening only to people whose opinions are like ours and spending time only with people whose experiences are similar to our own.

We need to broaden our minds and perspectives if we want to become more empathic. We need to get out of our own circles. And we need to seek out and embrace thinking different from our own. Professor Matthew D. Kim writes,

> Like most people, I enjoy reading books, journal articles, and reviews where I'm essentially told I'm right.... But as my colleague Scott M. Gibson has pointed out to me, the more we read the same authors, the same publishing houses, the same journals and magazines,... and the same news outlets, our thought universe shrinks.... Can we try to read one whole book this year from an author in another camp or with a totally different perspective? It may make us mad. We may disagree. We may absolutely hate the book. But... empathy emerges when we read and digest opposite perspectives, even when it may feel infuriating.[79]

It's difficult to place people ahead of our own agendas if we don't understand them or feel any empathy for them. When our hearts are softened, our minds are opened. When our minds are open, we are less likely to dismiss or overpower them to get our way.

2. Make Time for People Daily

It's important to have a heart for people, to care about them and value them. But it's also crucial to put that caring into action. The way to do that is to be intentional about making time for people every day. My favorite way to do that is what I call "walking slowly through the crowd." By that I mean I take my time and connect with people whenever I'm out in public. That may not sound like a big deal, but I'm a very impatient person who likes to get where he's going. Despite that, instead of rushing past people, I slow down and take the time to talk and interact with them. When I'm in the office, I stop and say hello to colleagues. Before and after I teach, I spend time off the stage chatting with attendees and taking pictures with them. As often as I can, I set aside a designated time to sign books for people after an event. And whenever I'm speaking at an event that includes a meal, I don't eat. Instead, while everyone else is eating, I use the time to visit every table and chat with people. The point of all these practices is to connect with people, to give them time and attention. If you want to be a high-road leader, take a detour. Get off your own agenda and spend time with people to connect with them because it demonstrates how much you value them.

I love a story Marilyn Gist tells about needing to find a speaker for an executive leadership program at Seattle University. She had set her sights on Jim Sinegal, co-founder of and at that time still CEO of Costco Wholesale. She wrote,

> I placed a phone call, prepared to share the planned date with his assistant and hear that Sinegal was unavailable. The phone

rang once, then a firm voiced answered, "Sinegal." I was stunned. What CEO of a very large, multinational firm answers his own phone?! I assumed he must have been expecting an important call and mine had interceded. Unprepared for this, I nervously explained who I was and that, although he didn't know me, I'd like him to speak to our class. He replied briskly, "What's the date again? What time? And what's your phone number? I'll have to check my calendar and get back to you." I was certain I was being handed off to an assistant, who would call back regretting Jim's unavailability to speak.

I'd begun wondering who else I could ask, when fifteen minutes later my phone rang. The voice on the other end said, "Marilyn, this is Jim Sinegal. The date looks OK. Where is it and what time do you need me there?" I was stunned again. He not only agreed to my request but had meant what he said about checking his calendar—then he personally called me back! Sometime later, on hearing me retell this story, Jim added, "Well, I don't always answer my own phone, Marilyn. But if I'm sitting there free, I do."[80]

From everything I've read about Sinegal, he has always made time for people. His agenda was never so important that he cut himself off from his employees or made anyone feel unimportant. He even made time for someone he didn't know like Marilyn Gist. That's quite a high-road accomplishment for someone leading a company with more than three hundred thousand employees that brings in well over $200 billion in revenue every year.[81] It's a good reminder that our work is never so big or so urgent that we should overlook or devalue people.

3. Check Your Agenda Repeatedly

In contrast, what happens when leaders put their agenda ahead of people? They can take their entire organization off course and create lasting damage to people. For example, in 2019, word went around the professional golfing world that an organization was forming a new tour to challenge the PGA. This kind of thing wasn't new. In fact, the PGA Tour itself had formed in 1967 when a group of players split from the PGA of America. And in the 1990s, there was an attempt to create a World Golf Tour. Now came a new challenger: LIV Golf Investments, and this time the effort was backed by Saudi Arabia's powerful Public Investment Fund, which had more than half a trillion dollars in assets.

What was the response of the PGA? The commissioner of the PGA Tour, Jay Monahan, warned that any PGA player who sided with a rival league by playing in its events would face suspension and possibly a lifetime ban.[82] The PGA also released statements harshly criticizing Saudi Arabia's human rights abuses against the LGBTQ community and women as well as its links to the Khashoggi murder and 9/11.[83] The Saudis were accused by critics of "sportswashing," investing large amounts in sports internationally to rehabilitate their poor reputation.

> Our work is never so big or so urgent that we should overlook or devalue people.

Why would golfers consider going to LIV? The organization was touting itself as a "player-focused alternative to the PGA Tour."[84] It intended to invest $200 million into the Asian tour, then create its own events that would pay players handsomely. The purses for competitors would be much larger than the ones in the PGA, no players would be cut from competitions, and even the player who finished last would take home $120,000.[85] In the PGA, a player who gets cut earns zero. In addition, to entice PGA golfers to join LIV Golf, the organization was offering huge incentives to sign on. Dustin Johnson initially said he was committed to the PGA, but he later resigned his tour membership to sign with LIV Golf for what's believed to be $150 million. "I don't want to play for the rest of my life," said Johnson, who is in his late-thirties. "This gives me an opportunity to do what I want to do."[86]

When players left the PGA and signed up for a LIV tournament, they were banned as promised.[87] Months later when Monahan was asked if he would lift the suspension on golfers who joined LIV if they wanted to return to the PGA, he said, "No. They've joined the LIV Golf Series.... As I've been clear throughout, every player has a choice, and I respect their choice, but they've made it. We've made ours."[88] Soon, attorneys got involved. A group of players sued the PGA. So did LIV. The PGA filed suit against them.

The lines had been drawn. There was no turning back. Or was there? Less than a year after Monahan said the PGA had made its choice, it made another choice. On June 6, 2023, Monahan announced the PGA would merge with LIV Golf.[89] Players who had stayed with the PGA Tour due to fear or loyalty had no warning and were stunned. So were the families of 9/11 victims who had supported the PGA's previous stance. In the end, the merger exposed the priorities of both organizations. The agendas of both the PGA and the Saudis were being preserved at the expense of people. The PGA wanted to keep its financial power and prestige, and Saudi Arabia wanted to improve its international profile using sports.

> **Anytime you work to accomplish your agenda at the expense of people, you're on the low road of leadership.**

Because it's so easy for leaders to become preoccupied by their own agendas, it's important for us to check our motives and our way of interacting with people every day. This reminds us of our priorities. Our actions may not be as far-reaching or hurt as many people as those of large and powerful organizations, but anytime you work to accomplish your agenda at the expense of people, you're on the low road of leadership.

4. Create Win-Win Outcomes Continually

The best way to place people above your own agenda and accomplish worthy goals as a leader is to consistently create win-win outcomes. Sometimes that can be difficult. But if you don't work to create a win-win, you'll almost always end up with a win-lose. Or worse, you may have to live with a lose-lose. Sadly, many leaders today are so bent on winning that when they realize they are going to lose, they work to make sure everyone else loses along with them. That's the lowest level of low-road leadership.

When you win at another person's expense, you're not only practicing low-road leadership; you're also engaged in short-term thinking. That inevitably prevents long-term success.

When you win at another person's expense, you're not only practicing low-road leadership; you're also engaged in short-term thinking. That inevitably prevents long-term success. Leaders who cause other people to lose to gain their own success always receive a lower return for their work over time. When people lose, they lose trust. They don't want to return to the table again. They avoid working with the low-road leader who made them lose. Then when a low-road leader wants to accomplish a new task or engage in another deal, they must seek out a new person who hasn't already been burned by them. As a result, their world shrinks, their network gets smaller, and the doors to new opportunities close ahead of them. In addition, the turnover on their teams or in their organizations grows, customers are harder to come by, and the cost of doing business goes up.

In contrast, when leaders create wins for everyone, people want to continue working with them. They remain on the team. They come back to the table to do other deals. That's why leaders who put people first are more successful in the long term. Creating wins for everyone builds momentum and makes winning more likely again in the future.

> Every person you work with has the potential to become an ally or an adversary depending on how you treat them.

Every person you work with has the potential to become an ally or an adversary depending on how you treat them. If you put them first and make sure they win along with you, they become allies. If you put your agenda first at their expense, they become adversaries. Don't short-change yourself by grabbing quick wins. Play the long game that comes from win-win.

DO THE LEADERSHIP DANCE

Placing people above your own agenda does not mean abandoning your leadership, nor does it mean relinquishing your vision. What's required is that you learn how to do what I call the *leadership dance*.

Leading people is never static. You must continually change the way you lead to fit the people and the situations, which are constantly shifting. This requires movement, rhythm, energy, and partnership. You must tune in to people's emotions and patterns of working. That's why I like to think of it as a dance. As you give people respect while accomplishing your goals, think about these five ways you can interact with them more effectively doing the high-road leadership dance.

Sometimes You're Ahead: Lead by Example

Sometimes the best thing you can do for your people is lead them from the front. You set the course for them. You face obstacles, challenges, and difficulties, breaking ground so that they can follow you. You face your fears, inspiring them with your efforts to draw them forward. This is the classic picture of leadership. It's what good military leaders have done for millennia.

Leaders are always setting the example because people do what people see. If you lead people, they are watching you, and they are most likely to follow you down the road you travel, whether it's low, middle, or high. So the direction you lead is important, but *how* you lead from the front also matters.

I have to admit, in the early days of my leadership, I wasn't sensitive to people. Every day with everyone it was the same: *Charge!* I was high in energy, ambitious, and determined to accomplish a lot. I didn't run over people or harm them to accomplish my agenda—I simply wore them out. It took me a while to learn that everyone was not like me and there was nothing wrong with that. After that, I started to learn the leadership dance and began adjusting the way I led each person and situation. And I tried to stay just a few feet ahead of people so they could see me. If you try to lead from miles ahead, the people get lost.

> When I finally understood that I couldn't lead everyone the same way, the first new skill I worked to develop was listening.

Sometimes You're Beside: Ask Questions and Listen

When I finally understood that I couldn't lead everyone the same way, the first new skill I worked to develop was listening. That was difficult for me because I'm a talker and a doer. Slowing down, asking questions, and giving people my undivided attention took a lot of effort and practice. But the payoff was huge. The best way to understand people is to listen. The best way to learn from others is to listen. The best way to receive people's best contribution is to listen. The best way to learn what others need from you is to listen. The best way to gain people's buy-in is to listen. Are you getting the picture? Listening gives you what you need to know to connect with people, meet them where they are, and keep them aligned with your agenda.

Sometimes You're Below: Serve Your People

One of the best things you can do for people you lead is to serve them. Obviously, this helps them. But it also does something more. Most people find it endearing when their leader contradicts the traditional image of leadership where the leader is over the people. It communicates to them their importance to you.

What are some of the ways a leader serves people? By removing obstacles no one else can. By providing resources they need. By lifting burdens off them that prevent them from being and doing their best.

Charlie Wetzel told me about a time early in his career when he worked at a junior college and got promoted from instructor to dean. While teaching, he and the other faculty members were required to perform various administrative tasks, which most of them found tedious, time-consuming, and annoying. Teachers want to teach; that's what they love. So when he became dean, he decided to take on those administrative tasks himself to serve his instructors and free them up to do what they did best. Many were grateful, but what really surprised Charlie was that he actually enjoyed doing it, largely because it served them.

> You can serve your people and still be their leader. You don't lose your position when you change your posture.

You can serve your people and still be their leader. You don't lose your position when you change your posture. Besides, real leadership isn't position anyway. It's influence. You can influence others from below just as easily as you can from above, and by doing that, you can help everybody win.

Sometimes You're Behind: Support Your People

Few things are more encouraging for people than being backed up by their leaders. Sometimes that support comes from being their advocate. Other times it's from giving them protection and security. But it always means helping them reach their potential. I've found three main ways to support people that I encourage you to adopt:

Pull Them Forward

OK, technically you don't pull someone forward from behind, but I use the word *pull* because it's really about drawing them forward. You pull people forward when you focus on their giftedness and are trying to help them grow. This kind of interaction comes from the heart. You can do this by approaching them with compassion to learn about their dreams, passions, and sense of purpose. You can help them by tapping into those things to motivate them. When I do this, I also try to help them develop their intuition and improve their timing. I want to help them improve themselves in their areas of strength so they can be their best. You can do that with people, too, as you support them.

Push Them Forward

When people need a push, it's usually in areas of choice. In these situations, it's often best to speak with candor and to challenge them. Help them to identify their values, tap into their sense of responsibility, honor their commitments, and increase their production. If their attitude is poor, challenge it, encouraging them to look for the good in the situation and to believe in themselves and their ability to succeed.

Sometimes challenging people is the only way to find out who they really are. When you push people to their limits, you find out what their limits are. I believe too many people limit themselves and sell themselves short. When challenged and encouraged at the same time, people find they can achieve much more than they believed possible. Pushing others is about helping them *perform* their best.

Patiently Wait for Them to Move Forward

Sometimes people are not yet ready to move. Perhaps they are dealing with great uncertainty. Or they lack experience in an area where they are expected to perform. Or they're in crisis. Or the timing for something to be accomplished isn't right. In those circumstances, the best support a leader can give is often to wait patiently.

I must admit, this is not something I enjoy, but it's often necessary. In times like these, I think of something Joyce Meyer said: "Patience is not simply the ability to wait—it's how we behave while we're waiting." As I wait, I try to take people through a process that helps them become ready to move forward, and then when they are, I discern whether they need a gentle push or pull.

> Pushing others is about helping them *perform* their best.

Sometimes You're Above: Advance the Big Picture

Leaders always carry the responsibility for seeing the big picture, communicating the vision, and putting people and resources in the right places for everyone to experience success. This is perhaps the best way you can serve your people and put them in the position to win. Does that mean you're pushing an agenda? Yes. But it's not a personal agenda for your own benefit. You're advancing a common agenda for the benefit of everyone. If you fail to identify and communicate the common vision for your organization or team, you create a void that someone else will try to fill. That runs the risk of the entire

PLACE PEOPLE ABOVE YOUR OWN AGENDA

team being sidetracked by another agenda and failing. If you're not communicating and advancing the big picture, are you really leading?

In the end, the best way to accomplish your agenda is to place people above it. That may feel counterintuitive, but it's true. If you serve the people you lead, they will serve you, just like if you do the right thing, that usually comes back to you. It's like a circle being completed. You can say, "What goes around comes around." You can believe it's karma. Or you can declare it's the Golden Rule coming to fruition. No matter what, it's a better way of treating people and accomplishing your goals as a leader.

> "Patience is not simply the ability to wait—it's how we behave while we're waiting." – *Joyce Meyer*

The Pathway to Placing People Above Your Own Agenda:
SERVING

To become a high-road leader who places people above your own agenda, you need to be willing to serve people. Too many leaders want to be the heroes in every interaction. They want to swoop in and save the day. They want to provide the solutions. They want to be the one to drop wisdom on everyone. High-road leaders make the people the heroes because it lifts them up. They are not only *willing* to serve their people—they *desire* to serve and support their people because they find enjoyment in seeing them succeed.

You will know you've begun to embrace serving your people when you find yourself asking questions such as, "What can I do to help them do their jobs well? How can I make sure they succeed? How can I serve them?" The best way for leaders to accomplish their work is to help their people succeed in theirs.

8

EMBRACE AUTHENTICITY

IF YOU DESIRE TO BE AN EFFECTIVE LEADER WHO TAKES THE HIGH road, then you must embrace authenticity. You can't hide. You can't pretend to be something you're not. You can't try to trick people into believing you are a better person or leader than you really are. You must be yourself with them—being open about your flaws and shortcomings as well as your strengths.

I admit that can feel scary. Once when I was speaking to a group of C-suite leaders, encouraging them to be open with their teams about their weaknesses, an attendee spoke to me afterward and challenged my thinking. He said he believed a leader should never show weakness to employees. "You're working under a misconception," I explained. "You think your people don't already know your weaknesses and flaws. The purpose of admitting them isn't to give them new information. It's to let them know that *you* know what they are."

BECOMING OPEN TO AUTHENTICITY

One leader whose openness and authenticity I admire is Jamie Kern Lima, the founder of IT Cosmetics. The tiny company she started in her living room in 2008 was bought by L'Oréal in 2016 for $1.2 billion.[90] Jamie has been very open and honest about her journey from being a young woman who overemphasized appearance, which included dieting in unhealthy ways since she was fourteen, to becoming someone working to change the beauty industry, pressing for the leaders of companies to stop promoting unrealistic and unobtainable standards of female beauty in advertising and media.

In her early twenties, Jamie became Miss Washington, was a contestant on the first season of *Big Brother*, and even appeared in an episode of *Baywatch* wearing the iconic red bathing suit. But her desire was to become a journalist. After earning an MBA from Columbia, she was hired as a morning TV anchor in Tri-Cities, Washington. But not long into her television career, she developed rosacea, an uncurable hereditary condition that caused hyperpigmentation, a permanent redness on the skin of her face.

"Everywhere I went were messages that love and approval were tied to appearance," she said, "so getting rosacea was confidence-killing."[91] Embarrassed, she covered her face with makeup, but she was unhappy with the results. "Every product I would find either wouldn't cover or products are so thick, they crease, they crack, they make you look older."[92]

That set Jamie on the road to creating better cosmetics. It was a struggle that nearly drove her into bankruptcy, but in 2010, she got a chance to go on QVC. She was determined to use herself and other women with flaws to display her products instead of beautiful models with perfect skin. She said, "In a moment on QVC, I took the plunge and went from being a girl who wouldn't leave the house without covering her face with layers of makeup to a girl who showed her naked, rosacea-filled, bright red face on national television."[93] That was the turning point for her business.

"Being vulnerable is hard," Jamie said, "but I've learned that sharing our true, flawed, authentic selves is the only way real connection and love can happen. It's the only way to step into our full power and purpose for our lives."[94] It's also the only way to become an effective high-road leader.

HOW TO EMBRACE AUTHENTICITY

For some people, being authentic is easy because they're naturally open books. But for most of us, it's a conscious choice we must make and continue to work on. If you desire to embrace authenticity and become more open, here are six things you can do that will help you.

1. Embrace and Live Good Values

It's much easier to be open with others when you're not trying to hide anything. People who say they believe in good values yet secretly live by a different set of values can't afford to be authentic because people will see the disparity, label them as hypocrites, and disrespect them. British novelist W. Somerset Maugham observed, "Hypocrisy is the most difficult and nerve-racking vice that any man can pursue; it needs an unceasing vigilance and a rare detachment of spirit."[95]

> "Sharing our true, flawed, authentic selves is the only way real connection and love can happen. It's the only way to step into our full power and purpose for our lives." – Jamie Kern Lima

The solution is to embrace good values and then do everything in your power to live them honestly and authentically. Sadly, in our world today, not only do many people espouse one set of values and live another, but we've experienced an erosion of values themselves. This means that people are unsure of what values are worth embracing, or they accept poor values as adequate.

Kevin O'Neill, a leadership guide at CEO-coaching firm Vistage, said that compromising your values in an effort to help others is analogous to moving a lighthouse. "A child, employee, or colleague may get lost in rough seas for a time," he said. "However, if they know where the lighthouse is, they can be guided back to safety. If the lighthouse has been moved, they may never find safe harbor."[96]

This "moving of the lighthouse" and decline of values has impacted society in nearly every way. Robert McKee, considered today's greatest expert on storytelling and screenwriting, says that even the stories we tell are affected by this:

> The final cause for the decline of story runs very deep. Values, the positive/negative charges of life, are at the soul of our art. The writer shapes story around a perception of what's worth living for, what's worth dying for, what's foolish to pursue, the meaning of justice, truth—the essential values. In decades past, writer and society more or less agreed on these questions, but more and more ours has become an age of moral and ethical cynicism, relativism, and subjectivism—a great confusion of values. As the family disintegrates and sexual antagonisms rise, who, for example, feels he understands the nature of love? And how, if you do have a connection, do you express it to an ever-more skeptical audience?
>
> This erosion of values has brought with it a corresponding erosion of story. Unlike writers in the past, we can assume nothing. First, we must dig deeply into life to uncover new insights, new refinements of value and meaning, then create a story vehicle that expresses our interpretation to an increasingly agnostic world. No small task.[97]

How do we recover from the confusion and decline of values? We intentionally and proactively identify the values that respect and cherish every human being, benefit others, and create a better society. Once we've done that, we accept those values, embrace them, and live them. That's the purpose of my nonprofit organization, the Maxwell Leadership Foundation, which exists to help people embrace and live the following values:

Attitude	Gratitude	Listening	Responsibility
Commitment	Hope	Love	Self-Regulation
Communication	Humility	Perseverance	Self-Worth
Courage	Initiative	Personal Growth	Servanthood
Fairness	Integrity	Priorities	Teachability
Forgiveness	Kindness	Relationships	Teamwork
Generosity	Leadership	Respect	Work Ethic

We are working to promote these positive values in several countries and in schools both in the United States and abroad. When our values, which are the principles that guide our decisions and behaviors, are good, they bring benefits—never harm—to ourselves and others.

Why was Jamie Kern Lima so willing to show her flaws to millions of people on national television? Because of her values. She wasn't living for herself. She was living to serve others. She loves people, particularly women, and she genuinely wants to help them live better lives. This comes from the core of who she is, and it has led her to become an advocate for them. In 2017 when she was asked to speak at the Cosmetic Executive Women Awards upon receiving the Achiever Award, she took the opportunity to challenge the titans of the beauty industry to include women of all shapes, sizes, ages, and complexions, not just young, thin models. "I believe the most beautiful women are real," she told them.[98] And she meant it.

"You can't fake authenticity," said Jamie. "If I said every woman was beautiful but was focused on my own insecurities, people wouldn't connect with me and I would fail. But I knew it wasn't about me; it was truly about something so much bigger. And because it wasn't about me, I became free."[99]

When your authentic self is flawed but operates according to good values, you're willing to show it to others. That frees you up to be yourself. At that point, if someone doesn't like you or agree with you, it's okay, because you are being true to yourself and your values. You can have the confidence of knowing you're doing what you believe is right, and you can live with your decisions.

2. Embrace the Idea of Living *between* Success and Failure

As leaders, we get in trouble if we internally label ourselves as a *success* or *failure*. If we define ourselves as successful, we may go into denial when we're leading or performing poorly. We may also try to cover up our mistakes because we don't want anyone to see evidence that contradicts our successful image. Defining ourselves as failures is equally problematic because people who see themselves as failures are defeated before they ever make the attempt to accomplish anything. What is the solution? Live between success and failure.

> When your authentic self is flawed but operates according to good values, you're willing to show it to others.

Here's how I visualize it. My life is like a road marked with lines at its edges. As I travel the road of leadership, the line on my right is success. When I'm near that line, everything seems to be going well. I'm winning and I feel successful. The line to my left is failure. When I'm close to that line, nothing seems to go right. I feel like I'm living Murphy's Law, where anything that can go wrong will go wrong—and at the worst possible time.

As I live my days, occasionally I'm moving along one of those lines because of what I do and who I am. On those days, I may feel one of these ways:

The Line of Failure	The Line of Success
I Feel My Weakness	I Feel My Strength
It Depresses Me	It Impresses Me
I Want No One to See	I Want Everyone to See
I Wish This Happened Never	I Wish This Were Forever
It's Me at My Worst	It's Me at My Best

While we all have times of success or failure, we usually live somewhere in the middle of the road. Those days when we're in the middle of the road walking, working, and leading are good days but imperfect days, and they define us—not our best days and not our worst. We need to be honest with ourselves and others about this because as my friend Craig Groeschel, the founder and leader of Life.Church, says, "People would rather follow a leader who is always real than one who is always right."[100] Authenticity is about living an open life between the lines.

> "People would rather follow a leader who is always real than one who is always right." – Craig Groeschel

Being your real self between the lines is empowering. It frees you up to be who you really are, to authentically connect with people, and to lead them with integrity. I like the way Jamie Kern Lima expresses this:

> When you hide important parts of who you are, you can't ever have authentic relationships. Because that other person is loving someone who isn't exactly you. We hesitate—what if they won't love us as we truly are? But then we have to ask ourselves what's worse—losing that person or losing the chance for true, authentic love the rest of our lives? We are

born with the need of human connection. So, if you've been scared to show up fully and authentically as the real, true you, then you are robbing yourself of that real human connection.[101]

Jamie wrote this while describing her closest friends, but the idea applies not only to friends and family but also to the people we work with and lead. Wouldn't you like to have unguarded, authentic relationships with people to help you live and lead better? I know I do.

3. Embrace the Value of Character Over Reputation

We live in a world where people focus too much on image and reputation. Individuals and organizations work hard to build brands. People present carefully curated versions of themselves on social media to garner likes and gain followers. But reputation has no substance, and images are often inauthentic. What really matters is character because that determines who you are, how you interact with people, and what you're capable of accomplishing. When your character exceeds your reputation, you can travel the high road even when it's difficult because your values and internal fortitude support you.

Some of my closest colleagues say that people often ask them what I'm really like. They want to see behind the curtain, and what they want to know is whether I'm the real deal, whether my internal character matches my reputation. That's a good question for me to ask myself every day. If my reputation exceeds my character, I'm in trouble!

I wrestled with this issue as a young leader. I had the desire to look better than I actually was. For a season, I wore glasses to look more intelligent. I grew a mustache to look more mature. I spoke on subjects others expected me to address, even though I didn't hold strong convictions related to them. As a result, when I communicated, my words did not ring true. That meant I was forfeiting whatever moral authority I had gained at that early stage of my career. I sensed that I needed to make a change. At the age of twenty-four, I made the decision to put my character first and align my actions and words with my beliefs. Alone in my study, I wrote the following words:

> "I will only teach what I believe." This gave me passion.
> "I will only teach what I experience." This gave me moral authority.
> "I will only teach what I live." This gave me authenticity.

Focusing on building character over reputation requires humility. Author and researcher Jim Collins described the humility of high-level, character-driven leaders as "compelling modesty." He said leaders focused on character pair lack of pretense with fierce resolve, modesty with willfulness, lack of personal ambition with fearlessness.[102] Those are all strong, positive character traits. They make it possible for leaders to live on the high road, lifting up others and their accomplishments instead of emphasizing their own.

> **People of good character have no reason to feel threatened by views different from their own.**

There's one more important strength people acquire when they develop good character. They are more able to respect others, listen to them, and understand their perspective. Why? Because people of good character have no reason to feel threatened by views different from their own. When people express opposing opinions, our natural tendency is to correct them, to put them in their place. That takes us off the high road. I must admit I did that too often in the past. But now, I check myself, challenge myself to listen, and respect the person and their view. That puts me back on the high road.

4. Embrace the Choices You Make Over the Gifts You've Been Given

At the 2016 Pathfinder Award in Seattle, Jeff Bezos, the founder of Amazon, was interviewed by Steve Taylor, the chief pilot for Boeing Flight Service. Asked about his quote, "Take pride in your choices, not your gifts," Bezos responded,

> This is something that's super-important for young people to understand, and for parents to preach to young people. It's really easy for a talented young person to take pride in their gifts. They say, "I'm really athletic," or "I'm really smart," or "I'm really good at math." And that's fine. You should celebrate your gifts. You should be happy. But you can't be proud of them because they're gifts, after all. They were given to you.
>
> What you *can* be proud of is your choices. How did you decide to use your gifts? Did you study hard? Did you work hard? Did you practice? The people who really excel combine gifts and hard work, and the hard work part is a choice. You get to decide that. And *that* is something that when you're looking back on your life, you will be very proud of.[103]

We have no control over our gifts. We have received what we have been given. We can't take credit for them.

> "Take pride in your choices, not your gifts." – *Jeff Bezos*

When I was a kid and brought home my report card, my parents looked at all of my grades. But there was one grade my dad always focused on. He said it was the most important one: effort. Even if my other grades weren't high, he was satisfied if my teacher reported that I had given A-level effort.

EMBRACE AUTHENTICITY

Talent is overrated. I've known talented people who did little with their lives and less talented people who went far. Haven't you? Furthermore, leaders who emphasize their talents and gifts to the people they work with separate themselves from others and often alienate them. High-road leaders avoid doing that. Instead, they connect with people, emphasizing what they have in common.

It's what we do with our talent that makes a difference. That's why several years ago I wrote a book called *Talent Is Never Enough*. I believe the positive choices you make will set you apart from those who have talent alone. These are the important choices you can make and how they maximize the gifts you've been given:

> The positive choices you make will set you apart from those who have talent alone.

    Belief Lifts Your Talent
    Passion Energizes Your Talent
    Courage Tests Your Talent
    Initiative Activates Your Talent
    Teachability Expands Your Talent
    Focus Directs Your Talent
    Character Protects Your Talent
    Preparation Positions Your Talent
    Relationships Influence Your Talent
    Practice Sharpens Your Talent
    Responsibility Strengthens Your Talent
    Perseverance Sustains Your Talent
    Teamwork Multiplies Your Talent

Every positive choice you make helps you to become a better person and a better leader.

5. Embrace the Value of Your Contribution

High-road leaders work at being self-aware and are able to realistically evaluate the contribution they make to their team, department, or organization. They don't overinflate the value of what they do to stroke their own egos. They don't undervalue their work because of insecurity. And they don't allow others to dictate what contribution they should make.

In her book *The Top Five Regrets of the Dying*, Bronnie Ware communicated what she'd learned while caring for people approaching the end of their lives. What was their number one regret? "I wish I'd had the courage to live a life true to myself, not the life others expected of me."[104] If you desire to be a high-road leader who embraces authenticity, you must be true to yourself and offer the world whatever you have to give, not what you wish you had.

> People's number one regret: "I wish I'd had the courage to live a life true to myself, not the life others expected of me."

What are the clues that you might not be valuing your contribution appropriately?

If You Often Seek Validation from Others

When you judge your contributions based on what other people think, you can become unstable. You no longer make decisions based on what you believe is right. You make them based on what others say. Maybe their standards are higher or lower than yours. Maybe they have another agenda. Maybe they say negative things because they're hurting or have terrible attitudes.

Don't allow others to steal your sense of identity or dictate your worth. Yes, sometimes getting feedback is good. So is getting advice from wise counsel. But if you live your life according to the opinions of others, you will become uncertain and superficial.

If You Often Compare Yourself to Others

Comparison can be a dangerous trap for any leader. The picture that comparison paints is always distorted. If you compare your worst to others' best, which is what everyone tends to show on social media, you feel terrible about yourself. If you compare their worst to your best, which is most people's natural inclination, you can get a swollen head.

Leadership speaker and consultant Adam F. Jones said, "Possibly the saddest thing about the cycle of comparison—and its ability to deter, delay and dissuade us from walking in our purpose and connecting to our core identity—is that it causes us to feel that we need to apologize for who we are. It causes us to lose the opportunity to connect and collaborate with others because we are consumed with feelings of inadequacy."[105]

If You Assume Your Contribution Isn't Enough

Another indication that you're not valuing your contribution is believing what you do or what you give is insignificant. Jones observed this among military veterans. When Adam F. Jones, a US Army veteran, connected with a store owner who had also served, the other man said sheepishly, "I was only a truck driver," as if his service wasn't enough. But Jones could relate to the other man's feelings. Jones himself had been a captain and a pilot of Black Hawk helicopters, a very prestigious duty. But after leaving the service, he tended to apologetically tell people he had never deployed.[106]

If you're a leader or team member working on a worthwhile goal, and you're contributing your best according to your strengths, abilities, and opportunities, you're doing your part. Don't minimize it.

When you value your contribution, it also empowers you to genuinely value the contributions of others, and you can make the most of your work together. That was true of Charles and Henry, two automotive pioneers who met in Manchester, England, on May 4, 1904. Charles was a twenty-six-year-old son of aristocrats. He had been educated at Eton and then attended Cambridge, where he studied mechanical engineering. He loved speed, had raced bicycles, and was the first undergraduate student to own a car. In 1900 he won the Thousand Miles Reliability Trial.[107] In 1903, he broke the world land speed record.[108] By that time, he was the best-known "autocarist" in Britain. He loved cars so much he set up a car importing and sales company with a partner, Claude Johnson. But he was frustrated. He wanted to sell cars made in England.

Henry, the other man at the meeting in Manchester, was forty, had been born into a poor farming community, and earned his way into a better life. At nine, he started selling newspapers and doing other odd jobs, but when he was fourteen, an aunt paid for him to become an apprentice with a railroad. There he discovered he had a knack for engineering, so he studied algebra and other subjects at night, which led to his landing a job with a power company. Later he started his own electrical engineering business. When Henry bought a used French automobile, he enjoyed it, but he believed he could build a better one himself. So he built a car with a powerful 10 horsepower engine, and he called it simply the Royce.[109]

The reputation of that car was what brought Charles Rolls to the meeting with Henry. As soon as Charles drove it, he fell in love with it and wanted to partner with Henry in a car company. In fact, Charles borrowed the car on the spot and drove it down to London. He woke up his car-selling partner, Claude Johnson, to give him a ride in it. That was the birth of Rolls-Royce Motor Cars.

The three men began working together and two years later, they produced their first car, called the 40/50hp. What made them successful was each of them knowing and valuing not only his own contribution but the contributions of the others as well. Henry

Royce designed and built the cars, and Charles Rolls didn't try to tell him how to do it, even though Rolls was the one with the engineering degree. Rolls promoted the company by driving the cars and winning races with them, and Claude Johnson didn't tell him how to do that, even though he had driven more hours than Rolls had. Johnson ran the company as managing director, becoming so crucial to its success that he came to be known as "the hyphen in Rolls-Royce."[110] An early ad for their first model, which came to be called the Silver Ghost, declared their goal: "The six-cylinder Rolls-Royce—not one of the best, but the Best Car in the World."[111] That claim was acknowledged as true back then. And many people today—more than one hundred years later—believe a Rolls-Royce is still the best car in the world.

If you desire to be your best and lead others to be their best, you need to value your contribution, work in your strengths, and lead everyone else on your team to do the same.

6. Embrace Honesty When You're Wrong or Make Mistakes

The final thing you can do to increase your authenticity so that you can lead on the high road is own your mistakes and be honest about them. People always respect leaders who openly admit when they are wrong and work to make things right.

As I was discussing this idea with my writing team while thinking about this book, Erin Miller spoke up about a meeting Mark Cole held with the leadership team of the Maxwell Leadership Company. To give you some background, a few weeks earlier, Mark and I had a conversation on a plane about the company. I thought we were going to talk about ways we could build the business. But the longer we talked, the more I sensed something was off. As CEO, Mark not only runs my companies, but he also is the primary carrier of my vision and legacy. In our meeting, I sensed that he was losing his way. We had a really hard conversation that day and then another one the next day. Mark realized he had been taking the staff and organization in a wrong direction.

Mark said, "I'm the steward of John's vision and tasked with expanding it. But because I had stopped bringing John in at key times, I'd missed too many things. When I realized it, I felt like I had failed my mission and disappointed my mentor."

Mark was very teachable, learned from the experience, and decided to set a different course for the companies. But that meant he needed to meet with the staff and reset expectations. At the meeting I mentioned, he told the leadership team he had failed, he had been leading them in the wrong direction, and that he and they needed to change. Then he said, "I've forgiven myself, and now I'm asking all of you to forgive me too."

> "Authenticity doesn't automatically guarantee success... but inauthenticity guarantees failure." – Jamie Kern Lima

Erin commented, "Mark was honest and vulnerable. I had more respect for him in that meeting than in any other we've ever had. The way he handled it was such high-road leadership to me. And I thought, *Wow. If I could learn to be that way, I would give myself and others much more grace and be able to move forward much more quickly.*"

I admire how Mark handled that with such authenticity and openness. He didn't try to fight for his rights. He didn't worry about his reputation. He was true to himself and his values. And he made choices that helped the company and his team. He took the high road.

When leaders look back on bad decisions, some rationalize what they've done. Some lie to themselves and others. Some fight. But if you're willing to be vulnerable, accept your mistakes and failures with grace, and learn from them, then you can move forward. And your team will come with you. People respect authentic leaders who take the high road. If you do anything other than embrace authenticity, people won't forgive. They won't jump on board with you and help you work through difficult situations. They'll stand by and watch you fail. What Jamie Kern Lima said is true: "Authenticity doesn't automatically guarantee success...but inauthenticity guarantees failure."[112]

The Pathway to Authenticity:
OPENNESS

If you want to lead on the high road, you need to become open about who you are—your weaknesses as well as your strengths. You must be open to admitting you're wrong or you don't know the answer. You need to be open to better ideas than your own and to the positive contributions of others. And you should become predictable in your calm but honest reactions to bad news and problems. A good place to start is by acknowledging your weaknesses and flaws to your team, as I suggested to the group of C-suite leaders. You can also ask people on your team what you're missing. If people respond in stunned silence or fail to point out anything you're doing wrong, take it as a sign that you have a long way to go to build trust with them, and the first step toward earning that trust is to become more open and authentic.

9

TAKE ACCOUNTABILITY FOR YOUR ACTIONS

I'M SURE YOU'VE HEARD THE EXPRESSION "THE BUCK STOPS HERE." It's a phrase President Harry Truman was known for. It came from a sign the president kept on his desk. I saw it when I visited the Truman Presidential Library in Independence, Missouri, many years ago. The sign's origin has an interesting story:

> The sign "The Buck Stops Here" that was on President Truman's desk in his White House office was made in the federal reformatory at El Reno, Oklahoma. Fred A. Canfil, then United States Marshal for the western district of Missouri and a friend of Mr. Truman, saw a similar sign while visiting the reformatory and asked the Warden if a sign like it could be made for President Truman. The sign was made and mailed to the President on October 2, 1945. . . .
>
> The saying "the buck stops here" derives from the slang expression "pass the buck" which means passing the responsibility on to someone else. The latter expression is said to have originated with the game of poker, in which a marker or counter, frequently in frontier days a knife with a buckhorn handle, was used to indicate the person whose turn it was to deal. If the player did not wish to deal he could pass the responsibility by

passing the "buck," as the counter came to be called, to the next player.[113]

President Truman was fond of this saying and referred to it in speeches on more than one occasion. In an address at the National War College in 1952, he said, "You know, it's easy for the Monday morning quarterback to say what the coach should have done, after the game is over. But when the decision is up before you—and on my desk I have a motto which says 'The Buck Stops Here'—the decision has to be made." And in his farewell address at the end of his presidency, he said, "The President—whoever he is—has to decide. He can't pass the buck to anybody. No one else can do the deciding for him. That's his job."[114]

> The better the excuse, the worse it is for us because we're more likely to let ourselves off the hook.

What Truman was describing was not only being responsible as a leader but also taking accountability. That's what we must do as high-road leaders. If we don't, we end up playing the blame game. We point to anything or anyone other than ourselves as responsible for anything that goes wrong. We expend our energy and creativity on finding good excuses. It would be wise for us to remember that the better the excuse, the worse it is for us because we're more likely to let ourselves off the hook.

What does it mean to take accountability for our actions? According to Michael Hyatt, here's what accountability looks like:

> First and foremost, it means that you accept responsibility for the outcomes expected of you—both good and bad. You don't blame others. And you don't blame the external environment. There are always things you could have done—or still can do—to change the outcome.

TAKE ACCOUNTABILITY FOR YOUR ACTIONS

Until you take responsibility, you are a *victim*. And being a victim is the exact opposite of being a leader.

Victims are passive. They are acted upon. Leaders are active. They take initiative to influence the outcome.[115]

You'll notice, in the title of this chapter, I suggest we *take* accountability, not *be accountable*. Why? Because this process is not passive. Accountability is active and intentional.

If you want to be a high-road leader, you can't pick and choose when you take accountability. To be considered accountable, you must demonstrate responsibility and ownership of your actions consistently, yet imperfectly. Accountability isn't a one-time occurrence. It's ongoing, so you are either accountable or you aren't. Professor Joyce E. A. Russell, former dean of the Villanova School of Business, advised, "Once you take the leadership job (or any job) you had better be prepared to deal with all of the issues, challenges and problems that arise and not just the easy ones. You should know this going into a position so that you shouldn't complain when it gets too tough."[116]

> **Take** accountability instead of *being accountable*. Why? Because this process is not passive. Accountability is active and intentional.

The sooner you take responsibility for your part anytime something goes wrong, the better. You need to become comfortable with the discomfort of being wrong and owning it. And like most things in life, the more you practice accountability, the better you will become at it.

INSIGHTS ON ACCOUNTABILITY

Many people avoid being accountable. Why? It's hard. It hurts. Nobody likes to admit being wrong. Nobody *enjoys* taking the blame or feeling responsible for failure. But accountability is one of the most important practices of good leaders. Here are some things you need to know about accountability in order to make it part of your life:

1. Accountability and Responsibility Work Together

Middle- and low-road leaders see their leadership position or authority as a benefit. They like the freedom of being in control, making decisions, and going to the front of the line. High-road leaders look at leadership as a responsibility. They pair that with accountability, which is a winning combination.

> "Responsibility is all *in the present*. Accountability is *after the fact*, which means owning the outcome—win or lose." – Gary Burnison

I like the way Gary Burnison, CEO of organizational consulting firm Korn Ferry, sees the relationship between accountability and responsibility: "Accountability is substantially different from responsibility. Responsibility is all *in the present*. Accountability is *after the fact*, which means owning the outcome—win or lose."[117]

Leadership and organizational behavior expert Jack Zenger said,

> Some might think that being responsible is the same thing as being accountable. But my later research suggests these are quite different mindsets. Being accountable means you are answerable and willing to accept the outcomes or results of a project or activity. But responsibility goes much further. It is the mindset that says, "I am the person who must make this happen," whether it stems from your belief or because your job requires this of you, or there is some social force binding you to this obligation.[118]

When I think about responsibility as a leader, I see it making an impact in three main areas:

Personal Responsibility

High-road leaders are first accountable to themselves. Gary Burnison said, "When most people think about accountability, they immediately look through the lens of how accountable others are to them. But first, we need to look in the mirror and see how accountable we are to ourselves—for who we are and how we act." He went on to say, "At the heart of accountability are two key principles: honesty and humility. With these 2 Hs, we become accountable for who we are—and who we become."[119]

One of the things my nonprofit leadership foundation does is teach students values in schools. One of the lessons we teach is on accountability. We want students to embrace that value because it helps them with so many other areas of their lives. Here is what we teach:

- We will keep our word. We will say what we mean and do what we say. We trust the word of others to be good as well.
- We will be on time. We will respect others by not wasting their time by making them wait on us.
- We will make things right. We will apologize, forgive, and ask for forgiveness.
- We will seek truth. We will discourage rumors and quickly work to separate facts from fiction.
- We will be mature. We will value the perspectives of others and resist seeing things only from our point of view.
- We will celebrate others. We will gladly point to and applaud the success of our peers.

- We will not make excuses. We will place responsibility on ourselves instead of blaming situations or others for our problems.
- We will look out for others. We will hold each other accountable because we want the best for others and ourselves.
- We will accept consequences. We understand that our actions or in-actions have consequences, and we will learn from them.

Personal responsibility is a success starter. When you accept responsibility for yourself, your problems, and your failures, you will be determined to find a way forward anytime you want to accomplish something. If you fail to take responsibility, you're more likely to find excuses, and excuses are success stoppers.

> **Personal responsibility is a success starter.**

If you want to be a high-road leader, then follow the advice of Gilbert Arland: "When an archer misses the mark, he turns and looks for the fault within himself. Failure to hit the bull's-eye is never the fault of the target. To improve your aim—improve yourself."[120] Take responsibility.

Team Responsibility

Anytime you are a member of a team, you have responsibilities to your teammates. I wrote about this in the Law of Countability in my book *The 17 Indisputable Laws of Teamwork*: teammates must be able to count on each other when it counts. If your teammates can't depend on you *all* the time, then they really can't depend on you *any* of the time. And that weakens the team.

I love how football coach Lou Holtz increased team responsibility among his players. He told me that the night before one of his bowl

TAKE ACCOUNTABILITY FOR YOUR ACTIONS

games, he had individual conversations with each player on his team and asked them the same question: "How can I count on you to bring us a victory?" The result was that players took responsibility and made themselves accountable for the outcome of the game. And they won.

I like teams that are up-front about team members' responsibility to one another and their commitment to results. Some teams use a creed, which the *Collins* dictionary calls "a set of beliefs, principles, or actions that strongly influence the way people live or work."[121] Recently I spoke for Optavia, a health and wellness coaching company. They talked about their Habits of Transformational Leadership, which I found inspiring:

> **Accountability is the glue that hold teams together, no matter how difficult circumstances become.**

> We awaken potential. We transform masterfully... We connect authentically. We cultivate trust... We seek growth. We embrace obstacles all the way... We take responsibility. We play above the line... We lead from the future. We act in the now... We deliver extraordinary results. We serve to better mankind![122]

These words emphasize their responsibility to the team and its mission. I really like that.

If you are part of a team, you must learn and embrace its values and make yourself accountable to your teammates. Accountability is the glue that hold teams together, no matter how difficult circumstances become. Either a team is pulling together, or it is pulling apart. Without a unified commitment to accountability, there isn't a team. So if you can't or won't take on that responsibility, you should leave and become part of another team.

Leadership Responsibility

Author Jack Zenger, CEO of the leadership development firm Zenger/Folkman, wrote about a study conducted by Dale Miller four decades ago that examined a pool of executives identified by their colleagues as effective and having the potential for promotion. After consideration, these leaders ended up falling into two groups. The first group was deemed ready to move up and the other was deemed unsuited for promotion after all. What made the difference? Zenger wrote,

> Each group received a deck of 62 statements describing management behavior. Each was asked to sort the deck in a forced choice, bell-shaped curve—going from the most effective to the least effective behavior. The highly effective group's top choice was the statement, "Accepts full responsibility for the performance of the work unit." This item was chosen far more frequently than statements about delegation, planning, staffing, time-management or technical skills. This choice also illustrated the sharpest distinction between the two groups. The managers who had been passed over for promotion attached far less importance to responsible behavior.[123]

If you want to lead a team effectively and remain on the high road, you must take responsibility for the team's performance.

The best way to do that is to focus on helping every member of the team reach their potential and work together to win. The best team leader I've ever known was John Wooden, legendary basketball coach of the UCLA Bruins. During one of our mentoring sessions, he told me, "There is a question I ask myself every day." As you can imagine, I could not wait to hear what it was. "Every day I ask myself, *How can I make my team better?*" That is the question every leader needs to be asking.

And whenever the weight of responsibility for leading people becomes too heavy, it's the leader's responsibility to redistribute the weight. Either some team members are not carrying their share of the load, or they need to be equipped to carry more and be held accountable to do it.

The good news for leaders is that taking responsibility and accountability makes them stand out, especially at a time when people want freedom and authority without taking on responsibility and accountability. The willingness to step up not only helps them accomplish what they set out to do; it also inspires others to follow suit. Author, speaker, and executive coach John Izzo wrote,

> "Responsibility is contagious. I call this the *responsibility ripple*. When someone steps up to change things, others step up and find courage they had not previously found." – *John Izzo*

> Responsibility is contagious. I call this the *responsibility ripple*. When someone steps up to change things, others step up and find courage they had not previously found.
>
> The responsibility ripple is an important principle because the moment we choose to act, the potential for a viral response is always there. Often, however, there is a need for one person, or a few, to be the catalyst that encourages others to step up.[124]

High-road leaders are willing to be those people and want to be catalysts for positive change.

2. Accountability Builds Your Credibility

The *American Heritage Dictionary* defines *credible* as "capable of being believed; believable or plausible."[125] The more accountable you are, the more credible you become. The greater credibility you demonstrate, the more believable and trustworthy you are to the people you lead.

In my book *The 16 Laws of Communication*, I teach the Law of Credibility, which states: "Your most effective message is the one you live." Why do I say that? Because talk is easy. Walking your talk is difficult. But if your life matches your talk and you take accountability for that consistency over the long haul, you develop more than credibility. You also develop authority, which is the highest level of credibility a leader can attain.

That doesn't mean you can rest on your laurels when it comes to credibility. You must earn it and re-earn it every day. In the book *Credibility*, authors James M. Kouzes and Barry Z. Posner write:

> Renewing credibility is a continuous human struggle and the ultimate leadership struggle. Strenuous effort is required to build and strengthen the foundations of working relationships. Constituents do not owe leaders allegiance. Leaders earn it. The gift of another's trust and confidence is well worth the struggle and essential to meeting the challenges of leading people to places they have never been before.[126]

Your accountable actions every day build your credibility with the people around you. Your behavior today is the latest deposit in your credibility.

Recently the coaching division of Maxwell Leadership was in talks with a group in Vietnam who wanted to create a partnership with us for a coaching certification process in their country. We discussed the details over several days, which culminated in a dinner with them so that we could make a decision. Mark Cole and I sat across the table from the three leaders who were proposing the partnership. At one point, one of the leaders said, "If we say it, we will do it. If we do it, we will do it well." Everything we knew about these leaders and our past dealings with them was consistent with what they said. That gave them credibility. And that sealed the deal.

3. Accountability Keeps You Consistent

My friend Mark Batterson said, "Almost anybody can accomplish anything if they work at it long enough, hard enough, and smart enough."[127] Do we have to work hard to be successful? Yes. Should we work smart? Absolutely. But the key is consistency. I've observed that long-term consistency is more powerful that short-term intensity. That's because consistency compounds. The Law of Consistency from *The 15 Laws of Growth* says, "Motivation gets you going—discipline keeps you growing." Taking accountability helps you become more consistent.

> **Your behavior today is the latest deposit in your credibility.**

I had the privilege of playing a round of golf with PGA professional Davis Love III. What a fantastic golfer. He has won twenty-one PGA Tour events, including the 1997 PGA Championship; captained the United States' Ryder Cup teams twice; and been inducted as a member of the World Golf Hall of Fame. As he and I played the course, I asked him lots of questions. One of the things he talked about stuck with me. He said that in the first round of a golf tournament, all the players have a chance to win. I admit, that seems pretty obvious. But, he said, by the fourth round, only about 25 percent of the players have a chance to win because most of them have been too inconsistent during the early rounds. Only the golfers who can sustain their level of play round after round have a chance to win in the end. "That's why they don't hand out trophies on the first day," he concluded right after hitting a long drive straight down the fairway.

When people are consistent, you can depend on them. You can trust them to follow through because their character will carry them forward, even when they're tired, frustrated, or overwhelmed. As science fiction author Robert A. Heinlein said, "Ability is a wonderful thing, but its value is greatly enhanced by dependability. Ability implies repeatability and accountability."[128]

4. Accountability Increases Your Self-Respect

My friend Chris Hodges, the founder of Church of the Highlands, likes to say, "Choices lead—feelings follow." When you make good choices and follow through on your commitments because you hold yourself accountable, the feeling that follows is self-respect. Your sense of self-respect will make you more self-confident. That in turn helps you make better choices uninhibited by guilt or doubt. It creates a positive cycle.

> "Choices lead—feelings follow." – *Chris Hodges*

It will also make a positive impact on others and your interaction with them. Bill Anuszewski, CEO of Jaywalker Lodge treatment center, said, "If you can keep commitments to yourself, you are likely to hold others to the same standards. You won't tolerate people who continuously blow you off because you know how important it is to stand by your word."[129]

One of John Wooden's favorite sayings was, "There is a choice you have to make in everything you do. So keep in mind that in the end, the choice you make, makes you."[130] Each time you choose to be accountable to yourself and others, you're making yourself into a better person and a better leader.

5. Everyone Needs to Be Accountable to Someone

You may have heard the famous quote by Lord Acton: "Power tends to corrupt and absolute power corrupts absolutely."[131] I agree with his observation. Now at age seventy-seven, I am more certain than ever before that everyone needs to be accountable to someone, because without accountability, we all tend to go off track and find ourselves on the low road of life.

When I was in my forties and I was gaining success as a leader, a mentor sat me down and said, "John, I don't trust you." He saw my reaction, but before I could object or plead my case, he said, "Calm down. I don't trust me either. We all need to be accountable."

I didn't like it, but I knew he was right. I must admit that I am my own greatest leadership challenge. That's why I've always loved this quote by President Theodore Roosevelt: "If you could kick the person in the pants responsible for most of your trouble, you wouldn't sit for a month."[132]

> **Do you know what I've discovered about improving myself? I do better when others help me do better.**

Are there places in your life where you're tempted to cut corners? Are there times when you want to take the easy way out instead of doing the hard thing you know is right? Are there areas of life where you would like to become better? I'm guessing your answer, like mine, is yes to one or more of these questionss. Do you know what I've discovered about improving myself? I do better when others help me do better.

When you welcome accountability, it benefits you in so many ways:

- You become aware of your blind spots.
- You're encouraged to take greater responsibility.
- You gain the wisdom of others' perspectives.

- You receive valuable feedback.
- You become more collaborative.
- You are more likely to create positive change.

Being accountable to someone else helps close the gap between intention and results. Each of us has so many good intentions. When we allow someone else to speak into our life, we are more likely to take action and follow through.

6. Saying No to Accountability Means Saying No to the High Road

If you desire to lead other people on the high road, you must embrace accountability. You must decide that the buck stops with you in your area of responsibility. Leaders who don't take accountability for their actions never gain the trust of their people, and because leadership is influence, it always functions on the basis of trust.

Academicians David Miller and Andrew Reeves studied how trust was impacted by the responses of two groups of elected officials following a crisis. The leaders in the first group passed the buck and blamed others. The leaders in the second group accepted the blame, therefore "stopping the buck." The evidence pointed in the direction we might expect. The leaders who took the blame were viewed more positively than the buck-passers, retained more public support, and were judged to have taken the superior strategy. Miller and Reeves concluded,

> Being accountable to someone else helps close the gap between intention and results.

In the Cherry Tree Myth, George Washington, a young boy, is said to have chopped down his father's cherry tree with his new hatchet. When Washington's angry father confronts him, the boy declares, "I cannot tell a lie... I did cut it with my hatchet." He eschews the natural temptation to blame someone else or feign ignorance and instead claims blame for the act. This national fable evokes admiration towards the first president because of his honesty and willingness to take responsibility for his peccadillo. It also encapsulates the findings of this research. Though there are costs for accepting blame and "stopping the buck," there are also reputational benefits. Just as Washington's father was likely pleased with his son, we find evidence that the public appreciates when elected executives claim blame for their actions.[133]

This is true not just for elected officials but for all leaders. Trust is the foundation of high-road leadership.

EVERYONE DESERVES TO BE LED WELL

Maxwell Leadership CEO, Mark Cole, created the motto of our companies, and I love it: "Everyone deserves to be led well." This is a truth that is universal. Everywhere I travel and speak, people *desire* good leadership, and they *deserve* good leadership. It's true in developing countries where leaders take advantage of the people. It's true in war-torn countries experiencing turmoil and distress. It's true in the capitals of Europe. It's true in the heartland of America. But do people receive good leadership in all these places? Do they receive high-road leadership? Rarely.

What makes the difference? How can all of us get the leadership we need and deserve? By holding ourselves and others accountable. If each of us would take accountability for our own actions, and we would require the people who lead us to do the same, the world would be transformed. Let's all take steps in that direction and see what happens.

The Pathway to Taking Accountability for Your Actions:
COURAGE

Many people struggle with taking accountability for their actions. It's human nature to avoid blame and conflict. It's always easier to hold back, keep a low profile, or hide than to step forward and face the consequences of what we've done. A lot of us have learned to be responsible and accountable from our parents. If we were held to that standard as children, we're more likely to uphold that standard ourselves as adults.

What if you have a difficult time taking responsibility? What if you find it difficult to own your actions or the results of your team? Can you change your behavior? The answer is yes. What it will take is courage. In moments when you want to remain silent, you will need to gather the courage to speak up. When your team fails, you must take the initiative to take responsibility for it with them and your superiors. When you're in conflict in a significant personal relationship, you must find where *you* are at fault, own it, confess it, and apologize.

At first, taking these actions will be difficult and uncomfortable. They may feel nearly impossible. But do it once, and the second time becomes easier. Do it in small things enough, and you will gain the courage to do it in larger things. And in time, it will become a normal, natural action you take. And it will put you on the high road.

10

LIVE BY THE BIGGER PICTURE

Have you ever wondered what all great leaders have in common? I have. In fact, I've spent more than a half century studying leadership and observing leaders, and I believe I have the answer. The distinctive ability of leaders is that they see more than others and they see before others. They possess a different perspective. They see the bigger picture, and they do so more quickly than others.

A DIFFERENCE IN PERSPECTIVE

Phil Geldart, an author and the founder of training company Eagle's Flight, compares the ability of leaders seeing the big picture to climbing to the top of a mountain and looking down at the valley below. He wrote,

> From this perspective you can see things clearly that may not have otherwise been so obvious; roads are not straight, homes and shops might not be ideally located. Going to the top gives you the ability to observe and correct or improve things that might otherwise be missed. It's an opportunity to ask yourself, *How can I make things better?*
>
> This exercise is imperative to organizational success, especially for those in positions of leadership. The need to see broadly like this is important to establish perspective, and in

turn judgment. Your judgment is based on how well you can keep the big picture view (the view from the mountain top) while executing against your day-to-day tasks (the valley).[134]

This ability to see from a broader perspective and understand situations within a larger context often has a profound impact on a person. Astronauts who have seen the earth from space have had their entire perspective on life changed. They experience what author Frank White termed the "overview effect." When astronaut Frank Borman first saw our planet from far away in 1968, he said, "What a view!" and, "This must be what God sees."[135]

More recently, actor William Shatner, who played the space-traveling captain of the USS *Enterprise* in *Star Trek*, got a chance to experience real travel into space, courtesy of Amazon founder Jeff Bezos. Journalist Marina Koren wrote about his reaction:

> When he first returned from space, William Shatner was overcome with emotion. The actor, then 90 years old, stood in the dusty grass of the West Texas desert, where the spacecraft had landed. It was October 2021. Nearby, Jeff Bezos, the billionaire who had invited Shatner to ride on a Blue Origin rocket, whooped and popped a bottle of champagne, but Shatner hardly seemed to notice. With tears falling down his cheeks, he described what he had witnessed, his tone hushed. "What you have given me is the most profound experience I can imagine," Shatner told Bezos. "It's extraordinary. Extraordinary. I hope I never recover from this." The man who had played Captain Kirk was so moved by the journey that his post-touchdown remarks ran longer than the three minutes he'd actually spent in space.[136]

I call this ability in leaders to see more and before the "leadership advantage." They have a perspective others don't have. People with high natural leadership gifting are born with this ability. However, even leaders who are not naturally gifted can acquire the ability to perceive the bigger picture so that they can also recognize and process situations more quickly than others around them. And this gives them a great advantage. The ability to see the bigger picture is like getting a thirty-yard head start in the one-hundred-yard dash. It enables heads of state to observe conflicts coming. It allows business leaders to notice problems and solutions before others do. It empowers entrepreneurs to recognize opportunities in the marketplace and seize them before anyone else can. Anyone who possesses the ability to see the bigger picture and uses it to take action can get a head start on others. That's why the race isn't always won by the fastest person; it's often won by whoever starts first.

> **This ability in leaders to see more and before is the "leadership advantage."**

Why is the big picture important for high-road leadership? Because it's like a superpower. And like any superpower, it can be used for good or ill. If you use this leadership advantage for good, you can help a lot of people by being a kind of real-life superhero. From your vantage point on the high road, you can see ahead and help people navigate the rough waters of life. You can lift them up when they're down. You can share opportunities you see and help them be successful.

When you live by the bigger picture, you increase your ability to make a difference in the lives of others. Just remember, as I said in chapter 4, your motives matter:

High-road leaders use the leadership advantage to help others.

Middle-road leaders use it to help themselves first before helping others.

Low-road leaders use it to help only themselves.

My hope is that you've already settled this issue and you're doing the right things for the right reasons.

There are also organizational benefits to seeing the bigger picture. BetterUp, an organization whose purpose is to facilitate transformation and peak performance in individuals, has studied the kinds of thinking that positively affect the future of organizations. As stated on their blog, Madeline Miles points out the great value in big-picture thinking, saying it provides organizations with five main benefits:

- **It helps organizations stay resilient in the face of change and adversity.** Big-picture thinking helps you build a cushion of resiliency amid change. When things throw you for a loop, your big-picture thinking can help you adapt with ease.
- **It keeps companies agile (especially during challenging times).** Agility is more important than ever with change as a constant. Especially when change becomes more complex, big-picture thinking keeps your company agile.
- **It helps improve your bottom line.** Adopting strategic thinking helps improve your organizational performance. When organizations are future minded, your overall performance benefits too.
- **It creates a culture of imagination and creativity.** At BetterUp, we value zest, playfulness, and imagination. When you're able to weave strategic thinking into your company culture, your employees benefit.
- **It can increase your organization's ability to adopt strategic foresight.** Strategic foresight is the ability to look ahead

and provide insight into what might happen in the future. This future-minded decision-making helps your organization stay ahead of the curve.[137]

If you want to help your organization, you need to be able to see the big picture.

ACQUIRING THE BIGGER PICTURE

How can you develop the ability to see the bigger picture so that you can use it to help others on the high road? Or if you already possess that ability to some degree, how do you sharpen and increase it? You can do it by focusing on growing in three ways:

1. Develop Maturity

It is nearly impossible to live by the bigger picture if you lack maturity. You can't be focused on yourself and travel the high road at the same time. By "maturity," I don't mean age. I know plenty of people who gain years yet lack the perspective and wisdom that come with maturity. One of the best descriptions of maturity I've ever read came from Pauline "Eppie" Lederer, the columnist better known as Ann Landers. In one of her most reprinted articles, she wrote:

> Maturity is many things. It is the ability to base a judgment on the big picture, the long haul. It means being able to resist the urge for immediate gratification and opt for the course of action that will pay off later. One of the characteristics of the young is "I want it now." Grown-up people can wait.
>
> Maturity is perseverance—the ability to sweat out a project or a situation in spite of heavy opposition and discouraging setbacks, and stick with it until it is finished. The adult who is constantly changing jobs, changing friends and changing

mates is immature. He cannot stick it out because he has not grown up....

Maturity is humility. It is being big enough to say, "I was wrong." And, when he is right, the mature person need not experience the satisfaction of saying, "I told you so..."

Maturity is the ability to harness your abilities and your energies and do more than is expected. The mature person refuses to settle for mediocrity. He would rather aim high and miss the mark than aim low—and make it.[138]

The hallmarks of maturity are humility, perspective, and patience. If we can be humble enough to understand the world is not about us, perceptive enough to recognize what's important, and patient enough to wait and play the long game for the best outcomes, we have the potential to live by the bigger picture.

2. Understand the Greater Context

A second ability that helps a leader to live by the bigger picture is seeing things within context. I gained insight on this idea several years ago when Margaret and I took a trip to Florence, Italy, to visit the art museums. Over the years, we've learned that on any trip, the guide makes all the difference. If your guide is great, your trip will be too. On this trip, we had an opportunity to be guided by the head of the art history department at Harvard. She made every piece of art we saw come alive to us.

Margaret is an artist, so she has a deeper understanding and keener appreciation for art than I have. As we started the tour with our guide, I was more excited for Margaret than myself. But within the first hour, my enthusiasm and appreciation took a giant leap forward. The guide gave context for every work of art by sharing the circumstances that surrounded its creation, the influences that shaped the artist, the history that preceded the work, and the impact it made. This showed me the importance of context for gaining understanding and clarity for the bigger picture, no matter the subject or circumstances.

This is especially true in leadership. Two leaders can work in the same field and possess the same goals, yet one will have clear vision for what could be and how to accomplish it, and the other may have no glimpse of the bigger picture. As German statesman and former chancellor Konrad Adenauer said, "We all live under the same sky but we don't have the same horizon." A leader who sees things in context sees more and before others.

> "We all live under the same sky but we don't have the same horizon." – *Konrad Adenauer*

Mark Cole, CEO and co-owner of Maxwell Leadership, and I work together every week discussing important decisions that must be made for the company. Most of the time we're exchanging information about the context. Why? Because good decisions are nearly impossible without context. After having hundreds of discussions with C-level executives, I believe I can help you develop seven contextual frameworks for seeing the bigger picture to help you lead on the high road.

Informational Context

We all have to begin somewhere. I start by asking for the basics. If I'm preparing for a speaking engagement, it starts with my executive assistant, Linda Eggers, who gathers the logistical details on the organization, date, time, and so forth. It continues with my pre-call to the host who has invited me so I can learn about their organization, expectations, and objectives. This gives me context I need to give my best. If I'm considering hiring a person, I want the basics on their character, areas of competence, and past work culture.

Historical Context

Knowing what happened in the past gives invaluable context for making decisions and taking action today. I discovered this truth when I was thirty-three years old and preparing to take over the leadership of a church whose founding pastor was retiring. I realized how much I needed to learn because he had started the church the same year I was born! To gain context before I started leading, I spent a week with the founder each month and gleaned as much information as possible about the organization. In those sessions I asked hundreds of questions. I wanted to know the highlights and low points in the church's history. I wanted to identify the main influencers and learn how they led. I wanted his opinions on what needed to change and what needed to stay the same. The more questions he answered, the more insight I gained into the bigger picture. A wise man once said, "Before you tear down the fence, ask why it was put there in the first place." That was what I was trying to learn.

> "Before you tear down the fence, ask why it was put there in the first place."

Situational Context

Just as important as historical context is situational context. By that, I mean what is happening and changing now, because that impacts what we want to do and the decisions we need to make. Sometimes you need to shift because of problems. But sometimes you need to make changes when conditions are good. My friend Dennis Rouse, founder of Victory World Church, says, "Leaders have to be willing to make changes when things are still going well, if they want to avoid decline." Good leaders remain flexible and agile, and they look at situational context to help them.

Motivational Context

As a young leader, I tended to inform my team about decisions I made without giving them the reasons behind them. Big mistake! As a leader, if you tell people what to do and not why, you get followers who don't think for themselves. They'll do the work, but when they're done, they will come back to you and wait for you to make the next decision. They want "boss help." If you want to develop leaders, then always give them the why behind every decision so that they see the bigger picture. Supplying that kind of context equips them to think for themselves and prepares them to lead others.

Collaborative Context

One of my favorite leadership practices is collaborating with good thinkers and leaders. I love discussing ideas and options with other people. It fulfills two of my greatest desires: connection and learning. Every time I do collaborative thinking, I learn something because I ask a lot of questions and do a lot of listening. I always benefit from the insights and innovation of others. When you include others in your conversation and thinking, it can't help but expand your perspective. Collaborative conversations always shape and enlarge the bigger picture.

> "Leaders have to be willing to make changes when things are still going well, if they want to avoid decline." – Dennis Rouse

Experiential Context

Once you've given the previous kinds of context your attention, it's time to use the context of your own experience to shine light on whatever you're trying to achieve. Your own experience has high value, but if you always use it as your starting point, you'll miss a lot, especially if you're older, as I am. Most people become progressively less open to new experiences as they age. They stop putting themselves into difficult or emotionally challenging situations. Instead, they seek out experiences similar to what they're used to, and as a result their picture stops expanding. Good leaders fight against limiting their vision because the broader and more varied the context they use, the greater their potential to see a bigger picture.

Tactical Context
Good leaders always have a plan. They go into any endeavor with a strategy. That's as true for army generals as it is for business CEOs or football coaches. However, great leaders know that when they execute their plan, the situation will change, and that will require changes in tactics. Any leader who fails to read the changing context and sticks too closely to their plan is destined to fail.

Changes in tactics because of context are easiest to see in sports because the game is played publicly, the time is compressed, and there is a score at the end of the conflict. One of the best coaches I've seen at reading the context and making adjustment is Nick Saban, former football coach at the University of Alabama. Whether his team was winning or losing at halftime, they came out of the locker room with a changed plan, and as a result, they usually scored more points or did a better job of shutting down their opponent's offense in the second half than they had in the first. As you lead others and step into "battle," you need to be ready to make adjustments too. Never stay so tied to your plan that you miss the bigger picture.

3. Become Highly Intentional About Seeing and Living the Bigger Picture
If you haven't always possessed the leadership advantage of seeing more and before, then you must make a conscious effort to look for the bigger picture continually in everything you do. That may not be

easy because of the demands of the world and the pace of life. As Phil Geldart said,

> When we get pulled in so many directions, with shifting priorities, and the never-ending pressure to produce results *now*, it can be difficult to step back, take a big-picture view and evaluate. However, the alternative is worse. You may wake up one day and find that what was is now no longer relevant, inefficient, or becoming less profitable. While it can seem difficult to find the time in a busy calendar to set aside for big-picture thinking, it is critical to the achievement of what is possible in the present and the future.[139]

In the last several years, I've gotten to know a leader who lives by the bigger picture. His name is Nido Qubein. He is one of the most intentional people I've ever met, and his story will not only inspire you to strive for high-road leadership but also teach you how to become more intentional about living the bigger picture. First, his story:

Nido grew up in Lebanon. When he was six years old, his father died. That meant he and his siblings were raised by their widowed mother. Though she was educated up to only the fourth grade, Nido's mother insisted that her children pursue education and even sent Nido, her youngest, to the United States for college. He arrived with fifty dollars, a few words of English, and a determination to succeed.

Nido earned an associate's degree from a community college, then a bachelor's degree from High Point College (now University), and later an MBA at the University of North Carolina. He started his career by creating a newsletter, which he sold and initially wrote himself. He used it to sell training materials. That grew into an award-winning public speaking career and an influential consulting business. Nido also wrote books. He ran other businesses. He helped start a bank. And he was asked to sit on many commercial and nonprofit boards, including BB&T, the La-Z-Boy Corporation, Dots Stores (fashion boutiques), and his alma mater, High Point University.[140]

In 2006, Nido received the Horatio Alger Award, presented to "exceptional leaders who have triumphed over adversity to achieve greatness."[141] He was highly successful, but what was to become his greatest success and contribution to others came as a surprise to him. When the president of High Point University (HPU) retired in 2005, the board pressed Nido to become the organization's new president. At first he was hesitant to take the role, but once he accepted it, his ability to see the bigger picture kicked in. He wanted to turn this small, little-known regional university into a world-class institution. And he is well on his way. Under his leadership, he has raised hundreds of millions of dollars. He has transformed the campus, having refurbished the original buildings, which he described as having had deferred maintenance; built forty-seven new buildings; and made the campus absolutely stunning. In addition, the university has increased its total enrollment from 1,673 to 6,000, full-time faculty from 108 to 353, campus size from 91 acres to 520 acres, square footage from 650,000 to 4.5 million, and operating and capital budget from $38 million to $378 million.[142]

With all those changes over nearly two decades, Nido has never lost sight of the bigger picture. He remarked, "Everything we did was focused on the student. We simply said, 'What can we do to insure that every student at High Point University receives an extraordinary education in an inspiring environment with caring people?' It's not complicated. It's amazing what happens when you focus on the student."[143]

What can you learn from Nido about becoming intentional in seeing and living the bigger picture?

Become Bigger on the Inside Than on the Outside

All his life, Nido has dedicated himself to personal growth and being true to his values. He has done the inner work needed to make him successful on the outside. His early years were filled with adversity and challenges. He had to learn English, and he was determined to master the language so that he could become a public speaker. He worked his way through school. When he launched his first business, he worked seventeen hours a day, seven days a week. His inner character made him strong and kept him going.

The best place to see the bigger picture is from a platform of success and significance. If you do the inner character work to become the best person and leader you can be, you will be able to achieve that perspective. And that will give you greater opportunities to lead others to success and significance yourself.

"Frame Your 'Masterpiece'"

This is a phrase Nido uses to help people keep their eyes on the bigger picture. What is your masterpiece? It's what you do best. It's your main contribution or your core business. What is the frame? It's what complements the masterpiece and takes it to the next level.

Nido's masterpiece at HPU is its academic programs. The university has fourteen schools, ten of which were created under Nido's leadership. More than $500 million has been invested in STEP programs, which include engineering, pharmacy, a biomechanics lab, and a planetarium. But what Nido believes takes the university to the next level is the way it teaches students life skills. He calls HPU "the premier life skills university" in the country. Faculty are required to include practical real-life application (often in community projects) in every course. They estimate that students and faculty perform half a million hours of service each year in the community. In addition, Nido teaches practical skills to students himself every semester.

Could HPU just teach life skills and be successful? No. The main thing is the academic curriculum. That's what students want to receive. Life skills merely enhance that as the frame.

How can you make a difference in the bigger picture? What is your masterpiece? What contribution can you make that will add value to your work, community, or the world? And how can you frame it to take it to the next level?

"Uplevel Added Value to Appreciated Value"

This is another phrase of Nido's. In the financial world, when people buy a piece of real estate, they hope its value will appreciate over time. That makes it a greater asset. That concept can also be applied to people. As leaders, we can add appreciated value to them, which has a multiplying factor. Appreciated value comes from giving people something of value plus finding out what they desire and adding that.

> Appreciated value comes from giving people something of value plus finding out what they desire and adding that.

One of the things that bothers Nido is how often parents work hard to give their children an education and send them off to a university, only to have their children come home with their values changed. He calls that educational malpractice. And he was determined that HPU would never be guilty of it. Its website states, "High Point University is a values-based institution. The values your family instilled in you for the last 17+ years will be furthered throughout your HPU education."[144] Nido calls this *appreciated value* because parents know that students will receive a fantastic education that equips them to pursue careers that make a difference in the world, plus the university will promote the values the parents embrace. Those positive values will help to sustain the students over the long haul.

How can you help others by not only adding value to them through your strengths and skills but by upleveling it to create appreciated value for them?

Choose to Become Distinctive—Not Just Different

Nido understands the power of being distinctive, not just different. Being distinctive means doing something that cannot be duplicated. What did he do at HPU to make it distinctive from other universities? Using connections from his long and successful career, he created what he calls his All-Star In-Residence Lineup. These are innovative people who help students. Here are just a few of the people in the group:

- Steve Wozniak, Apple Computer Co-founder
- Marc Randolph, Netflix Co-founder
- Cynt Marshall, CEO of the Dallas Mavericks
- Russell Weiner, Domino's CEO
- William E. "Bill" Kennard, former US Ambassador and Chairman of the Federal Communications Commission
- Dee Ann Turner, former Vice President for Talent at Chick-fil-A
- Byron Pitts, Co-anchor of ABC's *Nightline*
- Dr. Ellen Zane, former CEO of Tufts Medical Center

I also have the honor of being part of this group. Every year, HPU students have access to these leaders. What other university does that?

What can you do to be distinctive? What can you do that will set you apart as a leader? When I talked to Nido, he said what made me distinctive is the number of leadership books I've written. He believes I give "qualitative quantity"—high-quality content in high quantity. What is your distinctive? What can you do in high quality and quantity that no one else could duplicate?

Create an Environment That Brings Out the Best in People

When I walk across the campus at High Point, the first thing I'm struck by is its beauty. Thirty gardens have been planted around the campus. There are fountains everywhere. The benches lining the walkways around campus feature bronze figures of great people sitting on them, such as Abraham Lincoln, Albert Einstein, Mother Teresa, and Martin Luther King Jr., so that students can sit with them and be inspired. Quotes from great leaders and thinkers are set in the concrete and on walls. The university says, "Every inch of HPU's 520-acre campus is intentionally designed to support, motivate, teach, and inspire—even the art."[145] I know of no other place like it in the world.

> The faculty and staff fully support students and Nido's desire to "plant seeds of greatness in the hearts, minds, and souls of students."

It's a great physical environment, but it's also a fantastic relational environment. The faculty and staff fully support students and Nido's desire to, as he says, "plant seeds of greatness in the hearts, minds, and souls of students." Students support each other too. Every student receives a mentor to help them. And Nido himself spends time on campus talking with students. The way he connects with them reminds me of my dad and how he would walk slowly through the crowd at Ohio Christian University when he was the president. What environment are you creating to help people rise to their potential?

Nido Qubein inspires me. He lives by the bigger picture, and he is making his greatest contribution in his seventies. I admire him, and seeing him make a difference enlarges me and makes me want to make a greater impact for others too. I hope his story has done that for you.

Living by the bigger picture is seeing the world as it is, finding opportunities to help others become great, and using your skills, talents, and resources to help as many people as you can in the time that you have. If you're mature enough to focus on others and take the long view of making a difference, if you are willing to broaden your view so that you see every person and situation in their context, and if you become highly intentional in seeing how you can add value to people, you will be able to live by the bigger picture.

The Pathway to Living by the Bigger Picture:
PERSPECTIVE

What's the key to living by the bigger picture? It's perspective. Being a leader means being able to see more and before. However, being a *high-road* leader means seeing not for yourself but for others. That requires humility. If you are willing to use your vision to become bigger on the inside, frame your masterpiece, be distinctive, create a positive environment, and pursue your goals—all while maintaining your perspective and remembering that leadership is not about you—then you will be able to become your best self, but not *for* yourself. And you will be able to make a positive difference in the world. It doesn't have to be big. It just has to be for others.

11

DON'T KEEP SCORE

I CAME FROM SMALL BEGINNINGS IN MY LEADERSHIP CAREER. As I've mentioned, my first job was as the pastor of a tiny country church in Hillham, Indiana. I made eighty dollars a week. For us to make ends meet, Margaret worked three jobs. She taught kindergarten in the mornings, worked in a jewelry store in the afternoons, and cleaned houses on the weekends. We had just enough money to put food on the table, buy gas for our car, and pay our few bills.

So you can imagine how excited we were when a very successful businessman and his wife from our church invited us to go out to eat with them. Arnold was the number one lumber broker in southern Indiana. He and his wife picked Margaret and me up in their beautiful, spacious Lincoln Town Car with plush leather seats, and drove us twenty miles to the bigger town of Jasper because it had a restaurant.

"John, go ahead and order the most expensive thing on the menu," Arnold said. And I did. I ate a T-bone steak and a baked potato with all the fixings, followed by cherry pie. The food and the conversation were fantastic. Even better, Arnold invited us back again, and it became a regular practice. Every Friday, they took us to Jasper for dinner and it was the highlight of our week. Margaret and I both worked so many hours and had nothing, so it was like going to an oasis after being in the desert all week.

Margaret and I worked in Hillham for three years and three months. We loved our time there, but when I got the offer to lead one of the top-giving churches in the denomination, we knew it was time to move on to our next great challenge. After making the decision, we announced my resignation on a Sunday morning. It was emotional for us and the congregation because we loved the people and they loved us.

After the service as people came to thank us and wish us well, I noticed that Arnold was holding back, waiting to speak to us. When he finally approached us, he had tears in his eyes. He hugged me and started sobbing. Finally, he said, "How could you leave us after all I've done for you?"

His words cut deeply to my heart. I thanked him for all the wonderful things he had done, because I was truly grateful to him. But in that moment, it struck me: *he keeps score*.

I went home that night, and I couldn't sleep. I kept thinking about Arnold and what he said. He was a wonderful person, and I believed he had not been keeping score intentionally—until I did something that displeased him. I was only twenty-five years old at the time, and I didn't have a lot of experience or perspective. I had deeply disappointed him. He wanted me to stay, but I knew Margaret and I were supposed to leave. Had I used him? Was he using me? All I knew was that his words were like a weight on me. I felt guilty, conflicted, and trapped.

By the end of that night, I had come to a decision. I would never let that happen to me again. I would not allow another person's scorekeeping to limit my purpose or my leadership. For the next twenty-two years while I led churches as a pastor, I never allowed anyone to buy my meal. If I went to lunch or dinner with anyone, I paid. If I couldn't afford to pay, I didn't go. I wanted to put myself in a position where I was giving rather than taking so that I could lead without guilt or obligation. I was determined to take the high road as a leader, even when others didn't take the high road with me.

WHY YOU SHOULD NEVER KEEP SCORE

In chapter 5, I wrote about how important it is for high-road leaders to give more than they take. In hindsight, I recognize how much my experience with Arnold boosted my desire to become a giver more than a taker. But it also made me realize how negative keeping score can be. That's why I want to address it now. While the idea of giving more than you take is an encouragement to move up and always travel the high road, this chapter is an admonishment to stay away from moving down by scorekeeping, because keeping score will always lead you to the middle or low road. Avoid the temptation to keep the score "even" with others or to keep yourself ahead for the wrong reasons. Why? Because to be a high-road leader, you cannot keep score.

Keeping score may appear to be a way not to get behind in life. Or it may look like a way to get ahead in leadership. But the reality is that the practice drags us and others down. Here are six ways I've seen scorekeeping hurt people:

1. Keeping Score Puts Guilt on Others

When Arnold cried and said, "How could you leave us after all I've done for you?" I believe it was an expression of sincere emotion. I'm certain he wanted us to stay, and his words definitely made me feel guilty, but I'm not sure he was doing that intentionally.

Attempting to put guilt on another person is always a manipulative act. When leaders do something for others, keep track of it, and then try to use it as leverage to get what they want, it's always wrong. It is an attempt to get others to play "catch-up." Low-road leaders position themselves so that the other person *never* feels caught up and is always put in an inferior position. This kind of manipulation usually tries to prompt one of two emotional responses:

- Guilt—making people feel they *did* something bad.
- Shame—making people feel they *are* bad.

The first is an attempt to change people's actions, but the second attacks their identity. When we allow shame to affect our identity, then we feel unworthy, and its negative impact can be debilitating.

We and the people we interact with would be much better off if we could be more like the grandmother who was celebrating her sixtieth wedding anniversary. As her grandchildren gathered around her, one of them asked the secret to their successful marriage.

> When leaders do something for others, keep track of it, and then try to use it as leverage to get what they want, it's always wrong.

"When we first got married," she replied, "I decided I would take Grandpa's ten biggest faults and choose to overlook them."

"What were they?"

"Well, I never got around to writing them down," she replied, "so whenever he did something I didn't like, I just said to myself, *It's lucky for him that's one of them.*"

2. Keeping Score Creates Feelings of Unfairness

All the time that Margaret and I went to dinner with Arnold and his wife, I had no idea he was keeping score and that each time we accepted another dinner, I was racking up a debt I could not repay. Maybe I was naïve. I was an optimistic kid who had never found myself in a situation like that before. It seemed really unfair at the time.

If you're a leader who intentionally gives while keeping score so that you can later collect on the "debt," you're taking advantage of others, and they will feel manipulated. Even if you get what you want in the moment, you will burn bridges and damage relationships. People will not want to follow you because they won't be able to trust you. It's simply not worth it. And it's certainly not high-road.

3. Keeping Score Becomes an Act of Control

> Leadership is influence. *High-road* leadership is *positive* influence.

Many people keep score because they want to use it as an act of control. If anyone ever looked at you and said, "You owe me," then you can be sure they have kept score in order to control or manipulate you. In such cases, the person keeping score will go on to define what you need to do to settle the score, and you can be certain it will be on their terms and in their favor.

As followers, none of us want to be threatened, manipulated, or controlled. As leaders, we should never use those tactics to move people to action or get our way. Leadership is influence. *High-road* leadership is *positive* influence. To lead others well, we need to build relational connections with people, not use scorekeeping as leverage to control them.

4. Keeping Score Removes Gratitude by Poisoning Attitude

When I realized that Arnold had kept score, all the gratitude I had felt for all he had done for me and Margaret became tainted. What I thought had been given freely I discovered had strings attached. My unconditional gratitude for what I believed was unconditionally given became damaged. I saw Arnold differently. I started to feel a lot of negative emotions. I felt vulnerable, and I doubted myself and questioned whether I had made the right decision. But my doubt quickly turned to anger because I felt I had been manipulated. That made me want to defend myself. All these feelings undermined and lessened my gratitude and threatened to derail my leadership.

Many years later, one of my mentors Fred Smith Jr., told me something I'll never forget. He said, "Gratitude is a fragile emotion." I've found that to be true. It's very easy to lose our sense of gratitude and become sour or cynical. That's why I've always worked to remain grateful. When people lose their gratitude, their attitudes become negative. And a negative attitude never leads people anywhere they want to go. It's better to be positive and grateful and say thank you for whatever good you receive. As medieval theologian Meister Eckhart said, "If the only prayer you say in your entire life is thank you, it will be enough."[146]

5. Keeping Score Increases Emotional Baggage Too Heavy to Carry

If you are a leader, someone is going to hurt you. People you lead will disappoint you. They will question your judgment and the decisions you make. They will criticize you. Some may even betray you. What will you do with that hurt? You have a choice. You can carry it with you by keeping score, or you can let it go.

I was very fortunate when I had my experience with Arnold. Because of my upbringing, the positive attitude coaching of my father, and the unconditional forgiveness of my mother, I was able very quickly to process the hurt and frustration I felt because of Arnold's scorekeeping. As a leader, I have a strong sense of purpose. I have places to go and things to do, and I know if I carry a lot of baggage, it will weigh me down and keep me from accomplishing what I desire.

If you decide to keep score with people, it will be like carrying heavy suitcases with you everywhere you go. I learned the literal price of not packing light on a trip to Japan many years ago. It was early in Margaret's and my travel experience and long before luggage had wheels. Each of us packed two large suitcases for our trip. We didn't understand the problem we'd created for ourselves until we got to Tokyo, and we had to carry our bags from one end of the train station to the other. It almost killed us. Never again did we overpack like that.

Choosing to keep score in life means you will continuously carry your negative emotions and record of wrongs. From the moment you wake up in the morning, you'll be dragging them with you. Into the shower. On your daily commute. At your work desk. To dinner with friends or family. And back to bed when you go to sleep. And with each new wrong you collect or frustration you keep, the bags will become heavier. How exhausting! Make a better choice. Release those heavy bags and leave them on the low road so that you can travel light on the high road.

6. Keeping Score Breeds Entitlement

Finally, if we keep score and believe we are ahead of others on our own internal scorecards, we can begin to feel entitled. *Because I've given so much,* we think, *others should be giving back to me.* We come to believe we deserve what we aren't getting or don't have. Our interactions with people change. We resent always having to be the giver, and we wait for others to "make things even." Our relationships become more transactional. When we do experience the impulse to give, we ignore or resist it because we think, *It's not my turn. It's their turn,* and we don't do the good we felt prompted to do. We stop adding value. We stop giving. We stop placing people above our own agenda. We stop doing the right thing. Our thinking shifts to the middle road. If this mindset is left unchecked, we can find ourselves on the low road as leaders.

To stay on the high road, we need to focus not on what we deserve but on how we can serve. We need to embrace an idea expressed by writer and cartoonist Shel Silverstein in his poem "How Many, How Much." He said,

> How much good inside a day?
> Depends how good you live 'em.
> How much love inside a friend?
> Depends how much you give 'em.[147]

What our teacher told us when we were kids in school is really true: you get out of life only what you put into it. To live a high-road life, you need to focus on what you give, not what others have taken.

HOW NOT KEEPING SCORE BRINGS PEOPLE TOGETHER

In late 2023, I heard a high-road leadership story that's one of the best I've ever encountered, and it shows the power of not keeping score. It was told to me by Clem Sunter at an event in Dubai where we were both engaged as speakers. Clem is an interesting man. Born in England and educated at Oxford, he moved to South Africa and worked as a leader in the mining industry, eventually serving as chairman and CEO of Anglo American Central Africa, at one time the largest mining group in the world. Clem expected to spend his entire career there, but then something happened that changed not only his career but also the future of South Africa.

> To stay on the high road, we need to focus not on what we deserve but on how we can serve.

In the early 1980s, Anglo American was looking for better ways to do economic forecasting for their business because the 1970s had been so difficult. They asked an expert from Royal Dutch Shell to teach them a process called *scenario planning*, and Clem was so intrigued by it that he introduced the process to his company. But he also applied it more broadly. He and a team developed a model showing two possible pathways forward for South Africa as apartheid was coming to an end. They labeled them the "high road" and the "low road." The high road involved negotiating genuine shared government between white people and Black people, leading to economic growth and a developed country. The low road involved recruiting a few compliant Black representatives into a phony governmental system, leading to violent conflict and the country becoming what Clem described as a wasteland. He presented these scenarios to leaders across the country, including then president F. W. de Klerk and his cabinet.[148]

> "Blessed are those who can give without remembering and take without forgetting."
> – Elizabeth Bibesco

What's amazing is that Clem told me he also got to present his ideas about the high road to Nelson Mandela in January 1990, the month before Mandela was released from prison. It must have made a strong impression because Mandela and de Klerk worked together to dismantle apartheid, create free elections, and develop a true shared government. That was possible only because the two men refused to keep score or try to settle old ones.

HOW NOT TO KEEP SCORE

English writer and actress Elizabeth Bibesco said, "Blessed are those who can give without remembering and take without forgetting."[149] That's at the core of not keeping score. If you have that desire, then I suggest you follow these three pieces of advice:

1. Keep Track Without Keeping Score

By definition, "keeping score" means being in competition with others. People keep score to keep track of who is the winner and who is the loser. Keeping score is appropriate for games but not for relationships. At the same time, if you want to be a successful leader, how can you do that without keeping score? By keeping *track*.

Keeping track is about my behavior. Keeping score is about yours. Keeping track is about the management of my life, making certain that I do the right things for the right reasons. Keeping score is about the manipulation of your life, controlling you, fostering guilt, creating unhealthy comparisons, increasing emotional baggage, and prompting feelings of unfairness.

My greatest leadership challenge every day is leading myself. Keeping track helps me do that. It holds me accountable for what I'm doing before I try to hold you accountable for your actions. Keeping track helps me to improve. It prompts me to ask, *Am I a plus instead of a minus in your life? Am I lifting your load instead of being a heavy load? Am I making sure you win when I win?*

How can I be certain I'm keeping track and not keeping score? I look for positive outcomes. Keeping score doesn't usually produce them.

I like to think of keeping track as *give and forget*. I remember what I'm doing to add value to your life but forget what I receive. I'm keeping track of myself, not you. Why? Because you matter! You are much more valuable than the score.

2. Forgive Everyone—Because Everyone Needs Forgiveness

Ernest Hemingway, who was awarded the Nobel Prize for Literature, wrote a short story called "The Capital of the World" that opens this way:

Madrid is full of boys named Paco, which is the diminutive of the name Francisco, and there is a Madrid joke about a father who came to Madrid and inserted an advertisement in the personal columns of *El Liberal* which said: PACO MEET ME AT HOTEL MONTANA NOON TUESDAY ALL IS FORGIVEN PAPA and how a squadron of Guardia Civil had to be called out to disperse the eight hundred young men who answered the advertisement.[150]

While Hemingway was making a point about how common the name Paco was, he revealed a deeper truth. Everyone needs and wants forgiveness.

Forgiveness is not about keeping score; it's about losing count. High-road leaders forgive others without placing conditions on them. They make that choice because it not only releases the other person from any harm they have caused, but because it also releases the forgiver. Forgiveness allows you to be free from the nightmares of the past so you can reclaim your dreams for the future.

> **Forgiveness is not about keeping score; it's about losing count.**

In 1987, I wrote my fourth book, *Be All You Can Be*. I was very proud of it because I felt I was finally getting the hang of this book-writing thing. But then I got a call from my friend David Jeremiah.

"John, I just read *Be All You Can Be*," he said.

"You did?" I answered quickly, and then listened intently, waiting with great anticipation for the compliments to come.

"Your chapter on Joseph . . ." *Here they come!* I thought. "It came from my sermon."

I was stunned. As he explained, I realized what had happened. I'd received an outline of his message, and it was so good I filed it. But I neglected to write where it came from. Much later when I went looking in my files for ideas, I grabbed it and used it to write my chapter, not remembering it was David's. I felt terrible and I apologized immediately. His response? He forgave me and never mentioned it again. He could have kept score and held it against me, but he didn't. That's what high-road leaders do. He and I remain friends to this day.

3. Practice the Platinum Rule

No doubt you're familiar with the Golden Rule: treat others as you would like to be treated. I've referenced it several times in this book. But did you know there is such a thing as the Platinum Rule? That says we should treat others *better* than they treat us. This is the essence of not keeping score. Really, it's the essence of high-road leadership. It means not keeping a record of wrongs done to us, retaliating, or holding grudges. It means being kind to others, even if they are unkind or indifferent to us.

I like what Swedish scientist and inventor Emanuel Swedenborg said about this:

> Kindness is an inner desire that makes us want to do good things even if we do not get anything in return. It is the joy of our life to do them. When we do good things from this inner desire, there is a kindness in everything we think, say, want, and do.[151]

If you cultivate this inner desire to be kind and do good things for others no matter how you're treated, you can become a high-road leader.

THE GREATEST EXPERIENCE OF MY LIFE

I want to share with you the highest value of not keeping score with other people in your life. I learned it more than twenty-five years after my experience with Arnold and my determination not to be a scorekeeper. It occurred during the greatest experience of my life, which you may be surprised to learn was the night I had a heart attack.

On December 18, 1998, my company hosted its Christmas party at the 755 Club at Turner Field, what was then the Atlanta Braves' baseball stadium. It was a wonderful night of celebration with colleagues, friends, and family. After a fantastic dinner, a band played and everyone danced, including Margaret and me. She and I had taken ballroom dance lessons, so we were having a fantastic time.

> The Platinum Rule says we should treat others *better* than they treat us. This is the essence of not keeping score.

At the end of the party, I wasn't feeling very well, and I was sweating. I attributed that to the exertion of dancing—until I felt an excruciating pain in my chest that dropped me to the floor. I lay there gasping, feeling like an elephant was on my chest as I waited for an ambulance to arrive.

At the hospital, the doctors confirmed that I was having a heart attack. They gave me morphine, but the pain kept getting worse. And at one point, I asked them to level with me. I wanted to know if I was going to die, and the doctor's answer was, "If nothing changes and we can't get the heart attack to stop, then yes, you probably will die."

Obviously, things did change, and they were able to save me, otherwise I wouldn't be telling you the story. But in that hour of uncertainty, when they brought my kids in to say goodbye to me, and I got to tell them and Margaret how much I loved them, I felt a great calm. That's why I call it the greatest experience of my life. First,

I found out I wasn't afraid to die. I think many people of faith like me wonder how they will face death. I had heard stories of "dying grace," and to be honest, I didn't think I'd have that. But I experienced a peace that only God can give. And second, I had a moment when I wondered if there was somebody I needed to call to ask their forgiveness. Or anyone I needed to forgive that I hadn't. I wracked my brain, and I couldn't think of anybody. I'm sure there were people I'd hurt, because I'm as human as the next person, but as far as I could tell, my slate was clean because I kept short accounts, asked forgiveness when I'd done wrong, forgave without conditions, and hadn't kept score.

That's what I hope for you. I hope you can travel the high road and keep your slate clean by not keeping score. And I don't want you to have to face a near-death experience to give you perspective.

The Pathway to Not Keeping Score:
GRACE

How can we prevent ourselves from keeping score with others? I believe the key is grace. What do I mean by *grace*? Among the definitions listed, you will find *favor, good will, mercy, pardon,* and *clemency*.[152] None of us is perfect. All of us make mistakes and hurt other people. All of us would like to be extended grace, be forgiven, and be shown good will despite our faults. If we desire that for ourselves, why not extend it to others? That's what being a high-road leader is all about.

12

DESIRE THE BEST FOR OTHERS

WHEN I WAS IN COLLEGE, ONE OF THE PEOPLE WHO WAS HELD UP TO us as a model of compassionate, proactive leadership was Albert Schweitzer. He was a high-road leader—and what a talented person! He earned a PhD in philosophy, became an author, studied music, performed as an internationally recognized concert organist, was an expert on Bach, and became a licensed minister. And then in his late thirties he earned a medical degree so that he could become a medical missionary. He traveled to Lambaréné in what is now Gabon and built a hospital there. He served there from 1924 until his death in 1965, having expanded the hospital to thirty-five buildings and receiving the Nobel Peace Prize along the way.[153]

One of Schweitzer's quotes made a huge impression on me. He said, "I don't know what your destiny will be, but one thing I do know: the only ones among you who will be really happy are those who have sought and found how to serve."[154] Those words made me want to become a people-focused leader who made a difference in the lives of others. My early philosophy of leadership was symbolized by a saying I quoted a lot: "People do not care how much you know until they know how much you care." And to this day, it still represents how I feel about leadership. I believe high-road leaders always let their people know how much they care. Or as author Simon Sinek says, "Leadership is not about being in charge, but about taking care of the people in your charge."[155]

WHO WILL STEP UP TO THE HIGH ROAD?

The world needs more leaders like Schweitzer, people who desire the best for others and take action to follow through with that desire. Mary Kay Ash, the founder of Mary Kay Cosmetics, said it this way:

> We need leaders who add value to the people and the organization they lead; who work for the benefit of others and not just for their own personal gain. Leaders who inspire and motivate, not intimidate and manipulate; who live with people to know their problems in order to solve them and who follow a moral compass that points in the right directions regardless of the trends.[156]

> "I don't know what your destiny will be, but one thing I do know: the only ones among you who will be really happy are those who have sought and found how to serve." – Albert Schweitzer

We need more high-road leaders.

Many years ago I received an encouraging card from a member of my congregation with kind words on it. I don't know who sent it, but I was grateful for the encouragement at the time. I liked it so much that I included it in my book *Be a People Person*. I hadn't thought about it for years, but seeing it again, I believe it describes high-road leaders:

> When special people touch our lives then suddenly, we see
> How beautiful and wonderful our world can really be.
> They show us that our special hopes and dreams can take us far
> By helping us look inward and believe in who we are.

They bless us with their love and joy through everything
   they give.
When special people touch our lives they teach us how to live.[157]

The question is, How can you or I become a special person? How can we become more effective leaders on the high road? According to Tim Spiker, an author and the founder of The Aperio, a leadership development group, "Three fourths of your effectiveness as a leader comes from who you are, not what you do."[158] In his book *The Only Leaders Worth Following*, he describes that effectiveness as resulting from being inwardly sound and outwardly focused.[159] Here's how he defines *inwardly sound*:

> "Three fourths of your effectiveness as a leader comes from who you are, not what you do." – *Tim Spiker*

> Ideals such as personal disciplines, integrity, authenticity, health in all areas of life, self-awareness, a clearly understood sense of purpose, humility, emotional intelligence, and unconditional love all made the list. Such ideals are the foundation of what makes a well-developed human being. Apparently, they were also the foundation of what makes leaders exceptional.[160]

Spiker said his findings were confirmed by other research performed by consulting firm KRW. They found that companies saw much higher financial returns when they were led by leaders who rated high on integrity and responsibility, which Spiker identified as inward soundness; and forgiveness and compassion, which he identified as outward focus.[161]

No matter how you measure leadership effectiveness—whether by the number of people helped, the extent to which they are helped, the organization's impact, increased profit, or extended influence—the results come from elevating people and adding value to them because you want the best for them. People are what make every one of these outcomes possible.

BRINGING OUT THEIR BEST

The way to bring out the best in others is to first *desire* the best for others. This requires a shift in the way you think, the words you use, and the actions you take. Here's how this works:

1. Change Your Thinking

Everything begins with a thought. To paraphrase Ralph Waldo Emerson: "Life consists of what you are thinking about all day." How do you think about what's best? What are your desires?

> Low-road leaders desire the best for themselves.
> Middle-road leaders desire what's fair.
> High-road leaders desire the best for others.

As a leader, what do you want to be known for? Accomplishment? Wealth? Power? Success? Winning? I've given years of thought to this question, and I've concluded that I want to be known for desiring the best for others. I want more *for* people than *from* people. And I've shifted my thinking to be focused on how I can help others win instead of thinking about how I can win for myself.

> Be known for desiring the best for others.

I love what my friend Jeff Henderson said about this in his book *Know What You're For*. He wrote, "In a hypercritical, cynical world, one that is often known for what it's against, let's be a group of people known for who and what we're FOR."[162] The way he thinks about being *for* others is the way we should think. He continued,

> My favorite definition of the word *FOR* is "to be in favor of."
>
> Imagine a world where team members are in favor of one another. Imagine a world where churches are in favor of one another.
>
> Imagine a world where employers are in favor of employees, and vice versa.
>
> It sounds so simple. It's also so very rare.[163]

High-road leaders are rare, and one of the reasons is that they are *for* others. They desire the best for others. That's why they are able to bring people together in a world that divides. To be a leader who *does* these things, you must become a person who *thinks* this way.

2. Change Your Words

When you give your changed thinking expression, it does three things for you. First, it cements the ideas and makes them more established in thinking. The more you articulate

> "My favorite definition of the word *FOR* is 'to be in favor of.'" – *Jeff Henderson*

something you believe, the stronger it becomes. Second, it starts to create the shift from idea to action. And third, it begins to positively impact people. Words have power. As King Solomon, believed to be the wisest person who ever lived, said, "Words kill, words give life; they're either poison or fruit—you choose."[164]

When my daughter, Elizabeth, was a child, one of her favorite holiday activities was making a wish and breaking the wishbone, which she and I would do every year on Thanksgiving Day. Back then I was always looking for ways to create positive, uplifting experiences for her and my son, Joel, much as I do now with my grandchildren, and hope to do someday with great-grandchildren. Because I wanted the wishbone experience to be a win for Elizabeth, I stacked the deck in her favor. Once the wishbone dried out, I would bend one side of it to weaken it. Then I made sure to hold that weaker side as I offered it to her and we made our wishes so that she would always win.

After winning so many years in a row, one time she said, "Dad, I always win, so I never get to hear your wish. What was it?"

> The ultimate goal of desiring the best for others is to actually help them be their best.

I told her the truth: "My wish is for your wishes always to come true." It was a great chance for me to express my desire for her to experience life's best.

3. Change Your Actions

Several years ago, I authored a book called *Intentional Living*. The main reason I wrote it was to move people from positive thinking to positive actions. In it, I said,

> Poet Samuel Johnson is credited with saying, "Hell is paved with good intentions." Why would he say such a thing? Isn't it a positive thing to want to do good, to possess a desire to help others? My answer is yes. Having a heart to help people and add value to them makes you a better person. But if you don't act on it in an intentional way, it won't make a difference.[165]

The ultimate goal of desiring the best for others is to actually help them be their best.

Thomas Edison said, "I never perfected an invention that I did not think about in terms of the service it might give others.... I find out what the world needs, then I proceed to invent."[166] I love that sense of pragmatism and propensity toward action. The place in my life where I am most active in living out my desire for people to experience the best and become their best is in writing my books. It's been my good fortune to write books that people want to read for more than forty years, and as long as I'm still helping people, I will continue to write. My hope for you is that you embrace actions to help others experience their best.

> The reality is that each of us is either a plus or a minus in the lives of others. We add value or we subtract it. We give or we take.

WORDS AND ACTIONS OF HIGH-ROAD LEADERS

As a wrap-up to this book, I want to give you five specific ways you can align your words and actions to be the kind of high-road leader who helps others be their best.

1. "I Value You"—Affirming Words and Actions

You already know how important it is to value all people. That was the subject of chapter 2. The reality is that each of us is either a plus or a minus in the lives of others. We add value or we subtract it. We give or we take. We either make people feel like more and that they can do more, or we make them feel like less and we undermine them. High-road leaders continually work to be pluses and to add value. The most basic way to do this is to affirm people by telling and showing them you value them.

If we find and focus on people's worst, we will want to correct them. But if we find and focus on their best, we will connect with them. High-road leaders always place connecting above correcting. I like how my friend Dianna Kokoszka, one of the premier business coaches in the country, expresses this idea. She says, "People grow into the conversations they have around them." I know this is true because when I was a child, every morning before I went to school my mom prayed a short prayer with me containing positive and life-giving words. I didn't always appreciate it because I wanted to get into mischief. But I went to school every day knowing I was valued, and it often brought out the best in me when I was tempted to live out my worst. Speak affirming words to others, and you will see them respond positively.

2. "I Believe in You"—Encouraging Words and Actions

German poet, philosopher, and statesman Johann Wolfgang von Goethe once said, "When we treat people merely as they are, they will remain as they are. When we treat them as if they were what they should be, they will become what they should be."[167] The first and most important step toward success is the feeling that we can succeed. Believing in others builds their lives. It helps them see the possibility in themselves. And when they see the possibilities, those possibilities can become realities.

> High-road leaders always place connecting above correcting.

As I've already mentioned, the way I do this with people is what I call putting a "10" on their heads. I see everyone as a ten out of ten. I look for their potential and let them know I believe they can reach it. That encourages them to be their best. If you will look for the best in others, tell them you believe in them, and then follow through by supporting them with further encouragement, you will be amazed by how most people rise to meet your positive expectations.

3. "I Need You"—Empowering Words and Actions

I'm fortunate because I learned how empowering the words "I need you" can be when I was a senior in high school. I grew up playing basketball, and I was the captain of our high school team. Many times as our team broke the huddle before the start of the fourth quarter, Coach Neff would grab my arm to hold me back as my teammates went out on the floor, and he would say, "John, look at me. I need you to play big this quarter." I would nod, and he'd say, "I know you will."

I cannot describe to you how I felt when he would say that. I ran out on the court determined not to disappoint Coach Neff or to let my teammates down. When leaders express their belief in us and their need for us to perform, what do we do? We step up big-time.

Saying you need the talent, skills, and participation of someone you lead is not a sign of weakness. On the contrary, it shows the desire for collaboration and the value you place on other people. It communicates that you want to work together to accomplish more than either of you could on your own. When I ask a friend or colleague for advice and gain from their wisdom, it empowers them. As Henry David Thoreau said, "The greatest compliment that was ever paid to me was when someone asked me what I thought and listened to my answer."[168] When I communicate to my certified coaches that I need their help to make transformation in other countries a reality, they volunteer to train people in values roundtables because they are empowered to make a difference in the lives of others. When I invite the members of my writing team to collaborate with me on a book, I'm empowering them to add their ideas to mine and take them to a whole new level. When I tell the people who donate to my nonprofit organizations how I need them and that I couldn't accomplish our mission without them, I'm empowering their pursuit of significance.

> "The greatest compliment that was ever paid to me was when someone asked me what I thought and listened to my answer."
> – Henry David Thoreau

If you'll let people know how much you need them, they will help you and you will be able to share success and significance with them. That is empowering.

4. "I Want More *for* You Than *from* You"— Expanding Words and Actions

High-road leaders who desire the best for others always want more *for* their people than they want *from* them. And they take steps to deliver more to them. This is true even in the world of sports. One of the athletes I admired when I was growing up was Bill Russell, who was not only one of the greatest basketball players of all time but also a high-road leader. He played center for the Boston Celtics from 1956 to 1969 and also coached the team from 1966 to 1969. He won eleven NBA championships, was an all-star twelve times, and was MVP five times. The Celtics retired his jersey in 1972. Remarkably, on August 11, 2022, the NBA retired Bill Russell's number for the entire league, meaning no player for any team in the NBA would ever wear the number 6 jersey again.[169] That's the first and only time that has happened.

> "The most important measure of how good a game I played was how much better I'd made my teammates play." – Bill Russell

As incredible a player as Russell was, he was an even better leader because he expanded the beliefs and abilities of his fellow players. Russell said, "The most important measure of how good a game I played was how much better I'd made my teammates play."[170] Don Nelson, who played alongside Russell, said, "There are two types of superstars. One makes himself look good at the expense of the other guys on the floor. But there's another type who makes the players around him look better than they are, and that's the type Russell was."[171] Russell didn't play the game only for himself. He played for others. He wanted more *for* his teammates than he wanted *from* them. As a high-road leader, you need to share that same mindset.

5. "I Will Help You"—Serving with Words and Actions

One of the best things you can do for others is step forward to help them. This is especially valuable when you're willing to be the *first* person to help, because it demonstrates how much you care and means so much to the person being helped. I say this because I always remember the people who were the first to help me in my life:

- Margaret—As I mentioned, my wife worked three jobs so I could give all my time and attention to leading my congregation in my first church.
- Elmer Towns—He offered to become my first mentor because he saw potential in me when others did not. More than fifty years later, he still mentors me.
- Les Stobbe—When I decided to become an author, Les reached out to me and offered his help. Now ninety books later, I am still grateful that Les took a chance on this rookie.
- Dick Peterson—When I started my first company, Dick left a promising career at IBM to lead the team from his garage. He lifted a huge load off me.
- EQUIP Board—The nonprofit organization I started in 1996 was big on vision and small on finances. The members of my board put up all the money for expenses from their own pockets, and we took off. Today's board still pays for all the expenses so that 100 percent of all donations go to the cause.
- Larry—My brother mentored me in business and financial matters and has helped me invest money so that I could keep my focus on adding value to people.

- John Cage—This cardiologist offered his medical help months before my heart attack, and because he did, my life was saved.
- Mark Cole—He was first to assure me with words and actions that I would always be his first priority, and as CEO of all our companies, he has demonstrated that to be true.
- Linda Eggers—She was the first executive assistant to say she would be with me until I retired. Thirty-five years later we are still working together.
- Harvey Mackay—Over lunch I shared with Harvey that becoming a Horatio Alger member was on my bucket list. Harvey said, "I can make that happen." And he did!

I could fill pages with the names of additional people who were the first to help me. And there are many more people whose names I don't know. I am indebted to so many who gave me help when I needed it. As a high-road leader, you should be thinking continually how you can serve the people in your life. What kind of help can you give them that shows you desire the best for them?

6. "I Will Do What You Cannot Do for Yourself"— Enlarging with Words and Actions

The final way I suggest you help others experience the best is by doing things for others that they cannot do for themselves. This practice is perhaps the favorite thing I get to do with others because it helps to enlarge them. Poet and allegorist John Bunyan said, "You have not lived today until you have done something for someone who can never repay you."[172] I couldn't agree with that idea more.

So many people did things for me that I could not do for myself early in my career. When I was leading my first church, my brother, Larry, paid for me to take business classes at Northwood University.

When I was relatively unknown, Robert Schuller invited me to preach at the Crystal Cathedral, which gave me national exposure. Bill Bright put me on a speaking program with big names like Chuck Swindoll, Lloyd Ogilvie, and Chuck Colson. Victor Oliver, my editor at Thomas Nelson, gave me the idea to write *The 21 Irrefutable Laws of Leadership*, which became my first *New York Times* bestseller. I could go on and on. Every one of these experiences enlarged me.

> "You have not lived today until you have done something for someone who can never repay you." – *John Bunyan*

Knowing the significant impact enlarging experiences had on me, I made it my goal to provide them to others when I could. For example, Anne Beiler, the founder of Auntie Anne's pretzels, told me it was her dream to meet Truett Cathy. Because I know the Cathys, I arranged a dinner at my home so she could sit with him and ask questions. When I was planning how to celebrate my sixtieth birthday, I decided that instead of throwing a big party, I would host an experience each month and invite a small group of friends to go with me as my guests. That year we played golf in Ireland, attended the Super Bowl, experienced the NCAA Final Four, and went to the Kentucky Derby. It was fantastic. And I created an event that Maxwell Leadership hosts every year called Exchange. It's designed to create experiences people can't get on their own, like traveling by private train to Windsor Castle to dine with a member of the royal family or taking batting practice at Fenway Park in Boston.

What can you offer people that they do not have access to any other way? Who do you know that they should know? What knowledge or wisdom do you possess that you can share with them? It doesn't have to be expensive or extravagant. Whatever you possess that you can share with others to lift them up and help them be their best is worth sharing. As writer Beth Revis said through the protagonist of her science fiction novel *Across the Universe*: "Power isn't control at all—power is strength, and giving that strength to others.... A leader is someone willing to give his strength to others so that they may have the strength to stand on their own."[173]

> People can trace their successes and failures to the relationships in their lives.

In my book *Winning With People*, I teach that people can trace their successes and failures to the relationships in their lives. Don't you find that to be true? Our best and worst days involve people. How many of those bad days have come from interacting with low-road people? How many of the best days have come from high-road people?

You know you've been with high-road individuals when they have...

> Brought people together,
> Valued everyone,
> Acknowledged their humanness,
> Done the right things for the right reasons,
> Given more than they've taken,
> Demonstrated emotional capacity,
> Placed people above their own agenda,
> Embraced authenticity,
> Taken accountability for their actions,
> Lived by the bigger picture,
> Avoided keeping score, and
> Desired the best for others.

These are the kinds of people who bring out the best in everyone around them. They make a difference. And when these high-road people are also leaders, the difference they make is huge.

High-road leaders put others ahead of themselves. They live for the good of others. And here's what's wonderful: Chinese philosopher Confucius said, "He who wishes to secure the good of others has already secured his own."[174] Desiring the best for others will always bring out the best in you!

> "He who wishes to secure the good of others has already secured his own." – *Confucius*

Several years ago, I read the words of the late US Supreme Court justice Sandra Day O'Connor. Her message, which she delivered to graduates at Stanford University in 2004, inspired me to write this book:

> If we focus our energies on sharing ideas, finding solutions and using what is right with America to remedy what is wrong with it, we can make a difference. Our nation needs bridges, and bridges are built by those who look to the future and dedicate themselves to helping others. I don't know what the future holds, but I know who holds the future: It is you.[175]

Her words are as relevant today as they were two decades ago. The future belongs to you. I hope and pray you will take the high road and use your leadership to make your family, organization, community, and nation better. It is the only way we will be able to bring people together in a world that divides.

The Pathway to Desiring the Best for Others:
INTENTIONALITY

The pathway to desiring and creating the best for others is really the pathway for every step along the way of the high road, and that is intentionality. Nothing happens without it. You must go out of your way to make a way for others. You must be intentional about changing the way you think, the words you speak, and the actions you take. We can be intentional about getting up every morning and asking ourselves, *How can I do what's best for others?* We can live every day working to do what's best for others. And then we can ask ourselves every evening, *What did I do today to do what's best for others?* If all of us do these things, we can travel the high road and make the world a better place.

NOTES

1. Lee Rainie, Scott Keeter, and Andrew Perrin, "Trust and Distrust in America," Pew Research Center, July 22, 2019, https://www.pewresearch.org/politics/wp-content/uploads/sites/4/2019/07/PEW-RESEARCH-CENTER_TRUST-DISTRUST-IN-AMERICA-REPORT_2019-07-22-1.pdf, 40.
2. Maya Angelou, Facebook, July 18, 2016, https://www.facebook.com/MayaAngelou/photos/hate-it-has-caused-a-lot-of-problems-in-the-world-but-has-not-solved-one-yet-may/10154668897994796/.
3. JB Pritzker, "'Would an Idiot Do That': JB Pritzker's 'The Office' Commencement Speech at Northwestern University," June 12, 2023, Politics Etc., YouTube video, https://www.youtube.com/watch?v=uWPFDpOJEME.
4. Megan Brenan and Nicole Willcoxon, "Record-High 50% of Americans Rate U.S. Moral Values as 'Poor,'" Gallup, June 15, 2022, https://news.gallup.com/poll/393659/record-high-americans-rate-moral-values-poor.aspx.
5. Bill Haslam, *Faithful Presence: The Promise and the Peril of Faith in the Public Square* (Nashville: Nelson Books, 2021), Kindle, 53 of 221.
6. Exodus 21:23–25 NIV.
7. Attributed to Gandhi, but no specific reference can be found, "An Eye for An Eye Will Make the Whole World Blind," Quote Investigator, December 27, 2010, https://quoteinvestigator.com/2010/12/27/eye-for-eye-blind.
8. *Cambridge Advanced Learner's Dictionary and Thesaurus*, s.v. "take the high road," accessed July 13, 2023, https://dictionary.cambridge.org/us/dictionary/english/take-the-high-road.
9. Marilyn Gist, *The Extraordinary Power of Leader Humility: Thriving Organizations—Great Results* (Oakland, CA: Berrett-Koehler Publishers, 2020), 32.
10. C. S. Lewis, *The Weight of Glory: And Other Addresses* (New York: Harper Collins, 2009), Kindle, 46 of 193.
11. Ed Mylett and Jamie Kern Lima, "THIS Will Change Your Life w/ Jamie Kern

NOTES

Lima + HUGE Announcement!!!," June 20, 2023, in *The Ed Mylett Show*, podcast, https://www.edmylett.com/podcast/jamie-kern-lima-changeyourlife.

12 Gist, *The Extraordinary Power of Leader Humility*, 24.
13 Gist, 154.
14 Samuel Chand, "Others First," *AVAIL*, Summer 2023, 4, https://www.flipsnack.com/availleadership/avail-journal-issue-14-jermone-glenn.html.
15 Original source unknown.
16 Adapted from Source Unknown, "Isn't It Funny," *Personnel Information Bulletin*, Veterans Administration, August 1956, 19-20, https://www.google.com/books/edition/Personnel_Information_Bulletin/5br6sX_Z1M0C?hl=en&gbpv=1&dq=.
17 Dan Witters, "U.S. Depression Rates Reach New Highs," Gallup, May 17, 2023, https://news.gallup.com/poll/505745/depression-rates-reach-new-highs.aspx.
18 "Depression Facts and Statistics," Anxiety and Depression Association of America, November 2, 2020, https://adaa.org/understanding-anxiety/depression/facts-statistics.
19 Kristin Neff, *Self-Compassion: The Proven Power of Being Kind to Yourself* (New York: Harper Collins, 2021), Kindle, 749 of 5293.
20 Author unknown, Kim Gayner, *Reality 101: A "Must Have" Guide to Life and Life Skills Survival Manual* (Victoria, BC, Canada: Trafford, 2010), 260.
21 Jennifer Porter, "How to Move from Self-Awareness to Self-Improvement," *Harvard Business Review*, June 19, 2019, https://hbr.org/2019/06/how-to-move-from-self-awareness-to-self-improvement.
22 Tasha Eurich, "What Self-Awareness Really Is (and How to Cultivate It)," *Harvard Business Review*, January 4, 2018, https://hbr.org/2018/01/what-self-awareness-really-is-and-how-to-cultivate-it.
23 Eurich, "Self-Awareness."
24 Eurich, "Self-Awareness."
25 Gist, *The Extraordinary Power of Leader Humility*, 20.
26 Kristin Wong, "Why Self-Compassion Beats Self-Confidence," *New York Times*, December 28, 2017, https://www.nytimes.com/2017/12/28/smarter-living/why-self-compassion-beats-self-confidence.html.
27 Rob Dube, "What Leaders Can Learn from Self-Compassion," *Forbes*, October 25, 2021, https://www.forbes.com/sites/robdube/2021/10/25/what-leaders-can-learn-from-self-compassion.
28 Eurich, "Self-Awareness."
29 Stephanie Harrison, "What Does Self-Compassion Really Mean?" *Harvard Business*

NOTES

Review, December 12, 2022, https://hbr.org/2022/12/what-does-self-compassion-really-mean.

30. Wong, "Why Self-Compassion."
31. Anne Gherini, "What a Self-Deprecating Sense of Humor Says About Your EQ," *Inc.*, November 29, 2018, https://www.inc.com/anne-gherini/what-a-self-deprecating-sense-of-humor-says-about-your-eq.html.
32. Cindy Lamothe, "The Benefits of Laughing at Yourself, According to Science," *Shondaland*, June 22, 2018, https://www.shondaland.com/live/a21755063/benefits-laughing-at-yourself-self-deprecation-science-psychology.
33. Adam Grant, "A Key to Better Leadership: Confident Humility," *Knowledge at Wharton*, December 6, 2022, https://knowledge.wharton.upenn.edu/article/a-key-to-better-leadership-confident-humility.
34. Grant, "A Key to Better Leadership."
35. Grant, "A Key to Better Leadership."
36. Gist, *The Extraordinary Power of Leader Humility*, 142.
37. Eurich, "Self-Awareness."
38. Rahm Emanuel, "Rahm Emanuel on the Opportunities of Crisis," *Wall Street Journal*, November 19, 2009, YouTube video, https://www.youtube.com/watch?v=_mzcbXi1Tkk.
39. Mahatma Gandhi, *Young India*, September 6, 1920, 7, MKGandhi.org, https://www.mkgandhi.org/voiceoftruth/franchiseandvoters.htm.
40. "Marie Curie," The Nobel Prize, https://www.nobelprize.org/womenwhochanged-science/stories/marie-curie?keyword=x-ray.
41. Dale Carnegie, *How to Win Friends and Influence People: The Only Book You Need to Lead You to Success* (New York: Simon and Schuster, 2022), Kindle, 21 of 288.
42. Steve Magness, *Do Hard Things: Why We Get Resilience Wrong and the Surprising Science of Real Toughness* (New York: Harper One, 2022), Kindle, 69 of 308.
43. Matthew D. Kim, "How to Handle Toxic Friendships," *Christianity Today*, October 2023, 25, https://www.christianitytoday.com/ct/2023/october/handle-toxic-friend-ships-empathy-unity-conflict.html.
44. Michelle Nichols, "U.S. Billionaires Pledge Fortunes to Charity," Reuters, August 4, 2010, https://www.reuters.com/article/idINIndia-50629320100805.
45. "Frequently Asked Questions," The Giving Pledge, accessed September 27, 2023, https://givingpledge.org/faq.
46. Robert Fulghum, *All I Really Need to Know I Learned in Kindergarten: Uncommon Thoughts on Common Things*, 25th anniversary ed. (New York: Ballantine Books,

NOTES

      2003), 124 of 214, Kindle.
47 Luke 10:30–35 NIV.
48 Warren Buffett, "My Philanthropic Pledge," The Giving Pledge, accessed September 27, 2023, https://givingpledge.org/pledger?pledgerId=177.
49 Gist, *The Extraordinary Power of Leader Humility*, 83.
50 Gist, 85.
51 Gist, 98.
52 Melinda French Gates and Bill Gates, "Pledge Letter," The Giving Pledge, accessed September 27, 2023, https://givingpledge.org/foundingletter.
53 *Merriam-Webster*, s.v. "dysfunctional," accessed November 16, 2023, https://www.merriam-webster.com/dictionary/dysfunctional.
54 "Mental Health by the Numbers," National Alliance of Mental Illness, updated April 2023, https://nami.org/mhstats.
55 Richard Alan Krieger, ed., *Civilization's Quotations: Life's Ideal* (New York: Algora Publishing, 2002), 324.
56 Arlin Cuncic, "Victim Mentality: Definition, Causes, and Ways to Cope," Very Well Mind, April 4, 2023, https://www.verywellmind.com/what-is-a-victim-mentality-5120615.
57 Robert E. Quinn, *Deep Change: Discovering the Leader Within* (San Francisco: Jossey-Bass, 1996), 21.
58 David J. Schwartz, *The Magic of Thinking Big* (New York: Prentice Hall, 1987), Kindle, 67 of 309.
59 Og Mandino, *The Greatest Salesman in the World* (New York: Bantam, 1985), Kindle, 50 of 76.
60 Richard Jerome, "Charlton Heston 1923–2008," *People*, April 21, 2008, http://people.com/archive/charltonheston-1923-2008-vol-69-no-15.
61 Judith Orloff, "Strategies to Deal with Victim Mentality," *Psychology Today*, October 1, 2012, https://www.psychologytoday.com/us/blog/emotional-freedom/201210/strategies-deal-victim-mentality.
62 Toyin Crandell, personal correspondence with author, November 16, 2023.
63 Brian Tracy, "Forward," in Larry Markson, *Talking to Yourself Is Not Crazy: Change Your Inner Dialog Take Control of Your Life* (Blomington, IN: Balboa Press, 2011), xi.
64 Rosemarie Jarski, *The Funniest Thing You Never Said 2* (New York: Penguin Random House: Ebury, 2010), 224.
65 Original source unknown.

NOTES

66 Pat Williams, *Go for the Magic: The Five Secrets Behind a Magical, Miraculous Way of Life* (Nashville: Thomas Nelson, 1995), 23.

67 John Mason, *Know Your Limits—Then Ignore Them* (Tulsa: Insight International, 1999), 15.

68 Pat Williams with Jim Denny, *Coach Wooden: The 7 Principles that Shaped His Life and Will Change Yours* (Grand Rapids: Revell, 2011), 56.

69 John Mason, *Conquering an Enemy Called Average* (Tulsa: Insight International, 1996), 24.

70 Karen Weekes, *Women Know Everything* (Philadelphia: Quirk Books, 2007), 155.

71 Greg Smith, personal conversation with the author at Exchange event, Boston, MA, November 2, 2012.

72 Pat Riley, *The Winner Within: A Life Plan for Team Players* (New York: Penguin, 1993), 139.

73 Quoted in Marjorie Seaton, Rhonda G. Craven, and Herbert W. Marsh, "East Meets West: An Examination of the Big-Fish-Little-Pond Effect in Western and Non-Western Countries," *Self-Processes, Learning, and Enabling Human Potential*, Herbert W. Marsh, Rhonda G. Craven, and Dennis M. McInerney, eds. (Charlotte, NC: Information Age Publishing, 2008), 353.

74 Parker Palmer, *Let Your Life Speak* (San Francisco: Jossey-Bass, 2000), 30–31.

75 *Merriam-Webster*, s.v. "resilience," accessed November 11, 2023, https://www.merriam-webster.com/dictionary/resilience.

76 Michael Levy, "Results of the 1992 Election," Britannica, https://www.britannica.com/event/United-States-presidential-election-of-1992, accessed October 5, 2023.

77 Eliza Collins, "Did Perot Spoil 1992 Election for Bush? It's Complicated," *Wall Street Journal*, July 10, 2019, https://www.wsj.com/articles/did-perot-spoil-1992-election-for-bush-its-complicated-11562714375.

78 Luke 22:25–27.

79 Matthew D. Kim, "How to Handle Toxic Friendships," *Christianity Today*, September 11, 2023, https://www.christianitytoday.com/ct/2023/october/handle-toxic-friendships-empathy-unity-conflict.html.

80 Gist, *The Extraordinary Power of Leader Humility*, 46–47.

81 "Company Profile," Costco Wholesale, accessed October 9, 2023, http://costco2022ir.q4web.com/company-profile.

82 Joel Beall, "The LIV Golf Series: What We Know, What We Don't, and the Massive Ramifications of the Saudi-backed League," *Golf Digest*, June 8, 2022, https://www.golfdigest.com/story/saudi-golf-league-2022-primer.

NOTES

83. Mike Kelly, "'I Literally Feel Sick': 9/11 Families Rage at LIV-PGA Merger. But Money Talks," *USA Today*, June 8, 2023, https://www.usatoday.com/story/opinion/columnist/2023/06/08/pga-liv-merger-betrays-september-11-victims-families-saudi-arabia/70299583007.
84. Alan Blinder, Tariq Panja, and Andrew Das, "What is LIV Golf? It Depends Whom You Ask," *New York Times*, May 22, 2023, https://www.nytimes.com/article/liv-golf-saudi-arabia-pga.html.
85. Peter Scrivener, "LIV Golf—All You Need to Know About Saudi-Funded Series," BBC Sport, June 8, 2022, https://www.bbc.com/sport/golf/61732801.
86. Scrivener, "LIV Golf."
87. Elliott Heath, "PGA Tour Bans All LIV Golf Invitational Series Players, *Golf Monthly*, June 9, 2022, https://www.golfmonthly.com/news/pga-tour-bans-all-liv-golf-invitational-series-players.
88. Joel Beall, "Joy Monahan Delivers Clear, Blunt Response to LIV Players Who May Want to Return to the PGA Tour in the Future," *Golf Digest*, August 24, 2022, https://www.golfdigest.com/story/jay-monahan-liv-golfers-tour-championship-2022.
89. Kevin Draper, "The Alliance of LIV Golf and the PGA Tour: Here's What to Know," *New York Times*, June 7, 2023, https://www.nytimes.com/2023/06/07/sports/golf/pga-liv-golf-merger.html.
90. A. Khan, "L'Oréal Buys IT Cosmetics for $1.2 Billion," *Allure*, July 25, 2016, https://www.allure.com/story/loreal-buys-it-cosmetics.
91. Jamie Kern Lima, *Believe It: How to Go from Underestimated to Unstoppable* (New York: Gallery Books, 2021), 28.
92. Khan, "L'Oréal."
93. Kern Lima, *Believe It*, 28.
94. Kern Lima, xi.
95. "W. Somerset Maugham 1874-1965, English novelist," *Oxford Essential Quotations, 4th ed.*, Susan Ratcliffe, ed. (Oxford: Oxford University Press, 2016), https://www.oxfordreference.com/display/10.1093/acref/9780191826719.001.0001/q-oro-ed4-00007179.
96. Kevin O'Neill, personal email to author, December 7, 2023.
97. Robert McKee, *Story: Substance, Structure, Style, and the Principles of Screenwriting* (New York: Regan Books, 1997), 17.
98. Jamie Kern Lima, "IT Cosmetics CEO Calls Out Beauty Industry, Calls for Change," IT Cosmetics, September 15, 2017, YouTube video, https://www.youtube.com/watch?v=tqRw-JSYADc.

NOTES

99 Kern Lima, *Believe It*, 28.
100 Craig Groeschel, "The Developer's Dark Side," *Craig Groeschel Leadership Podcast*, August 1, 2018, YouTube video, https://www.youtube.com/watch?v=5NGYwhO-Q6UY&t=31s.
101 Kern Lima, *Believe It*, 88–89.
102 Jim Collins, "Level 5 Leadership: The Triumph of Humility and Fierce Resolve," *Harvard Business Review*, January 1, 2001, https://hbr.org/2001/01/level-5-leadership-the-triumph-of-humility-and-fierce-resolve-2.
103 Jeff Bezos, "Jeff Bezos Shares His Management Style and Philosophy," GeekWire, October 28, 2016, YouTube video, https://www.youtube.com/watch?v=F7JMMy-yHSU&t=7s .
104 Bronnie Ware, *The Top Five Regrets of the Dying: A life Transformed by the Dearly Departing* (Sydney: Hay House, 2019), vii of 305, Kindle.
105 Adam F. Jones, "The Cycle of Comparison: Relish the 90% You Have Versus the 10% You Don't," *AVAIL*, Summer 2023, 72, https://www.flipsnack.com/availleadership/avail-journal-issue-14-jermone-glenn.html.
106 Jones, "The Cycle of Comparison," 71.
107 Richard Cavendish, "The Birth of Rolls Royce," *History Today*, May 5, 2004, https://www.historytoday.com/archive/birth-rolls-royce.
108 "How Rolls Met Royce," Rolls-Royce Motor Cars, accessed December 1, 2023, https://www.rolls-roycemotorcars.com/en_US/inspiring-greatness/values/how-rolls-met-royce.html.
109 "How Rolls Met Royce."
110 "How Rolls Met Royce."
111 "How Rolls Met Royce."
112 Kern Lima, *Believe It*, 106.
113 "'The Buck Stops Here' Desk Sign," Harry S. Truman Library Museum, accessed December 4, 2023, https://www.trumanlibrary.gov/education/trivia/buck-stops-here-sign.
114 "'The Buck Stops Here.'"
115 Michael Hyatt, "How Real Leaders Demonstrate Accountability," Full Focus, accessed December 4, 2023, https://fullfocus.co/leadership-and-accountability.
116 Joyce E. A. Russell, "Great Leaders Don't Pass the Buck," *Forbes*, September 26, 2020, https://www.forbes.com/sites/joyceearussell/2020/09/26/great-leaders-dont-pass-the-buck.
117 Gary Burnison, "Owning the Outcome," Korn Ferry, accessed December 6, 2023,

NOTES

https://www.kornferry.com/insights/special-edition/owning-the-outcome.

118   Jack Zenger, "Taking Responsibility Is the Mark of Great Leaders," *Forbes*, July 16, 2015, https://www.forbes.com/sites/jackzenger/2015/07/16/taking-responsibility-is-the-highest-mark-of-great-leaders/?sh=521fbc2d48f2.

119   Burnison, "Owning the Outcome."

120   Gilbert Arland, quoted in H. Jackson Brown, Jr., ed., *A Father's Book of Wisdom* (Nashville: Rutledge Hill Press, 1988), 115.

121   *Collins English Dictionary*, s.v. "creed," accessed December 5, 2023, https://www.collinsdictionary.com/us/dictionary/english/creed.

122   "Coaching Guide for the Habits of Health Transformational System," Optavia, accessed December 6, 2023, https://optaviamedia.com/pdf/learn/50107_GUI-OPTAVIA-Coaching-Guide-for-the-HOH-Transformational-System.pdf.

123   Zenger, "Taking Responsibility."

124   John Izzo, *Stepping Up: How Taking Responsibility Changes Everything,* 2nd ed. (Oakland, CA: Berrett-Koehler Publishers, 2011), 333 of 3342, Kindle.

125   *The American Heritage Dictionary of the English Language*, s.v. "credible," accessed December 6, 2023, https://www.ahdictionary.com/word/search.html?q=credible.

126   James M. Kouzes and Barry Z. Posner, *Credibility: How Leaders Gain and Lose It, Why People Demand It* (San Francisco: Jossey-Bass, 2011), 198 of 250, Kindle.

127   Mark Batterson, *Win the Day: 7 Daily Habits to Help You Stress Less and Accomplish More* (Colorado Springs: Multnomah, 2020), 15 of 235, Kindle.

128   Source unknown.

129   Bill Anuszewski, "5 Reasons Why Keeping Commitments Will Make You a Better Person Overall," Jaywalker, October 18, 2016, https://jaywalkerlodge.com/5-reasons-why-keeping-commitments-will-make-you-a-better-person-overall.

130   John Wooden and Steve Jamison, *Coach Wooden's Leadership Game Plan for Success: 12 Lessons for Extraordinary Performance and Personal Excellence* (New York: McGraw-Hill, 2009), 5.

131   "Power and Authority," Lord Acton Quote Archive, Acton University, accessed December 6, 2023, https://www.acton.org/research/lord-acton-quote-archive.

132   "Six Powerful and Wise Quotes from Theodore Roosevelt, *Business Insider*, September 16, 2012, https://www.businessinsider.com/six-powerful-and-wise-quotes-from-theodore-roosevelt-2012-9.

133   David Miller and Andrew Reeves, "Pass the Buck or the Buck Stops Here? The Public Costs of Claiming and Deflecting Blame in Managing Crises," *Journal of Public Policy* 42, no. 1 (March 2022): 63–91, https://www.davidryanmiller.com/

NOTES

files/main-rr.pdf.
134 Phil Geldart, "The Importance of Seeing the Big Picture," *Entrepreneur*, April 30, 2020, https://www.entrepreneur.com/leadership/the-importance-of-seeing-the-big-picture/349368.
135 Jeffrey Kluger, "The 'Overview Effect' Forever Changes Some Astronauts' Attitudes Towards Earth—But You Don't Need to Go to Space to Experience It," *Time*, July 30, 2021, https://time.com/6084094/overview-effect.
136 Marina Koren, "Seeing Earth from Space Will Change You: The Question is How," *The Atlantic*, January/February 2023, https://www.theatlantic.com/magazine/archive/2023/01/astronauts-visiting-space-overview-effect-spacex-blue-origin/672226.
137 Madeline Miles, "6 Big Picture Thinking Strategies that You'll Actually Use," BetterUp, July 19, 2022, https://www.betterup.com/blog/big-picture-thinking.
138 Ann Landers, accessed December 13, 2023, "Maturity Means Many Things," *Chicago Tribune*, July 17, 1999, https://www.chicagotribune.com/news/ct-xpm-1999-07-17-9907170129-story.html.
139 Geldart, "The Importance of Seeing."
140 "Nido R. Qubein," The Horatio Alger Association of Distinguished Americans, Inc., https://horatioalger.org/members/detail/nido-r-qubein.
141 "Horatio Alger Award," Horatio Alger Association of Distinguished Americans, Inc., https://horatioalger.org/horatio-alger-award/.
142 "High Point University—High End Marketing at Its Best?" Wally Boston, February 15, 2023, https://wallyboston.com/high-point-university-high-end-marketing-at-its-best.
143 "Nido R. Qubein: A Life of Success and Significance," High Point University, October 25, 2013, YouTube video, https://www.youtube.com/watch?v=g-bJEu898sNA .
144 "Values at High Point University," accessed December 13, 2023, High Point University, https://www.highpoint.edu/values.
145 "Experiential Learning," High Point University, accessed December 14, 2023, https://www.highpoint.edu/experiential-learning.
146 Maggie Oman Shannon, *The Way We Pray: Prayer Practices from Around the World* (Berkeley: Conari Press, 2001), 76.
147 Shel Silverstein, "How Many, How Much," *Light in the Attic* (New York: Harper Collins, 1981), 8 of 101, Kindle.
148 Clem Sunter, *Flag Watching: How a Fox Decodes the Future* (Cape Town: Tafelberg,

NOTES

2015), 61 of 2279, Kindle.

149 Michael W. Foss, *Real Faith for Real Life: Living the Six Marks of Discipleship* (Minneapolis: Augsburg Books, 2004), 110.

150 Ernest Hemingway, "The Capital of the World," *The Complete Short Stories of Ernest Hemingway*, Finca Vigía Edition (New York: Scribner, 2003), 29 of 652, Kindle.

151 Larry Chang, ed., *Wisdom for the Soul: Five Millennia of Prescriptions for Spiritual Healing* (Washington, DC: Gnosophia, 2006), 137.

152 *Webster's New Universal Unabridged Dictionary*, 1996, s.v. "grace."

153 "Albert Schweitzer Biographical," NobelPrize.org, accessed December 15, 2023, https://www.nobelprize.org/prizes/peace/1952/schweitzer/biographical.

154 "Albert Schweitzer Quotes," Brainyquote.com, accessed December 15, 2023, https://www.brainyquote.com/quotes/albert_schweitzer_133001.

155 Source unknown.

156 Glenn Elliott and Debra Corey, *Build It: The Rebel Playbook for World-Class Employee Engagement* (Chichester, UK: Wiley, 2018), 77.

157 Original author unknown, quoted in John C. Maxwell, *Be a People Person: Effective Leadership Through Effective Relationships* (Colorado Springs: David C. Cook, 2007), 11.

158 Tim Spiker, *The Only Leaders Worth* Following: Why Some Leaders Succeed, Others Fail, and How the Quality of Our Lives Hangs in the Balance* (Atlanta: Alperio Press, 2020), 13 of 228, Kindle.

159 Spiker, *The Only Leaders Worth* Following*, 30 of 228.

160 Spiker, 30 of 228.

161 Spiker, 33 of 228.

162 Jeff Henderson, *Know What You're For: A Growth Strategy for Work, an Even Better Strategy for Life* (Grand Rapids: Zondervan, 2019), 21 of 254, Kindle.

163 Henderson, *Know What You're For*, 125 of 254.

164 Proverbs 18:21 MSG.

165 John C. Maxwell, *Intentional Living: Choosing a Life that Matters* (New York: Center Street, 2015), 27.

166 "Thomas Edison Quotes," ThomasEdison.com, accessed December 16, 2023, https://www.thomasedison.com/quotes.html.

167 "If We Treat People as If They Were What They Ought to Be, We Help Them Become What They Are Capable of Becoming," Quote Investigator, October 9, 2018, https://quoteinvestigator.com/2018/10/09/capable.

NOTES

168 "Henry David Thoreau Quotes," Brainy Quote, accessed December 16, 2023, https://www.brainyquote.com/quotes/henry_david_thoreau_132515.

169 "Bill Russell's No. 6 Jersey to Be Retired Throughout NBA," NBA.com, August 11, 2022, https://www.nba.com/news/bill-russells-no-6-jersey-to-be-retired-throughout-nba.

170 Robert W. Cohen, *The 40 Greatest Players in Boston Celtics Basketball History* (Camden, ME: Down East Books, 2017), 8.

171 "Legends Profile: Bill Russell," NBA, September 13, 2021, https://www.nba.com/news/history-nba-legend-bill-russell.

172 John Bunyan, *The Poetry of John Bunyan: Volume II,* (Portable Poetry, 2017), 1 of 1072, Kindle.

173 Beth Revis, *Across the Universe* (New York: Razor Bill, 2011), 223 of 260.

174 "Confucius," *Dictionary of Quotations,* James Wood, ed. (London: Frederick Warne & Co., 1899), Bartleby.com, accessed December 15, 2023, https://www.bartleby.com/lit-hub/dictionary-of-quotations/authors/confucius-5.

175 Sandra Day O'Connor, "Full Text of Justice Sandra Day O'Connor's Commencement Address," Stanford, June 13, 2004, https://news.stanford.edu/2004/06/13/full-text-justice-sandra-day-oconnors-commencement-address

ABOUT THE AUTHOR

JOHN C. MAXWELL IS A #1 *NEW YORK TIMES* BESTSELLING AUTHOR, speaker, coach, and leader who has sold more than thirty-six million books in fifty languages. He is the founder of Maxwell Leadership®—the leadership development organization created to expand the reach of his principles of helping people lead powerful, positive change. Maxwell's books and programs have been translated into seventy languages and have been used to train tens of millions of leaders in every nation. His work also includes that of the Maxwell Leadership Foundation and EQUIP, nonprofit organizations that have impacted millions of adults and youth across the globe through values-based, people-centric leadership training.

John has been recognized as the #1 leader in business by the American Management Association and as the world's most influential leadership expert by both *Business Insider* and *Inc. Magazine*. He is a recipient of the Horatio Alger Award and the Mother Teresa Prize for Global Peace and Leadership from the Luminary Leadership Network.

Maxwell and the work of Maxwell Leadership continue to influence individuals and organizations worldwide—from Fortune 500 CEOs and national leaders to entrepreneurs and the leaders of tomorrow. For more information about him and Maxwell Leadership, visit maxwellleadership.com.

Maxwell Leadership Certified Team

Earn a Living Helping Others Lead.

We are looking for leaders with a true commitment to lead through positive influence. Is that you?

Become a part of our global community of leaders, influencers, and high achievers who are making a difference by developing leaders right in their community.

The Maxwell Leadership Certified Team is global community of Maxwell-certified leadership development professionals who are trained and qualified to speak, coach, train and facilitate Maxwell Leadership programs. Our Certified Team members are entrepreneurs and business owners in every industry. We have members in over 160 countries, but what really ties us together is a genuine commitment to lead through positive influence. That's our #1 value: to be agents of powerful, positive change in the lives of others.

At the foundation of every Certified Team member's business is a comprehensive curriculum based on the leadership values and principles of John C. Maxwell, making the Maxwell Leadership Certified Team program the top leadership development certification in the world.

Are you ready to chart your own course, at the helm of your own business? When you become a Maxwell Leadership Certified Team member, you are 100% in control of your own business, earning income on your own terms... it pays to be the boss! And you won't be doing it alone. You'll be a part of a global community of over 50,000 Maxwell Leadership Certified Speakers, Coaches and Trainers, led by our expert team of mentors and faculty, including John C. Maxwell. You'll have access to the people, tools and resources you need to build a thriving leadership development business.

If you're looking for greater influence and impact with the support of a proven business model and a team of faculty and mentors led by John C. Maxwell, we invite you to join our winning Team!

SCAN THE CODE
TO LEARN MORE

Learn more at
maxwellleadership.com

Do you have an unstoppable desire to make a difference in the lives of people?

I've always dreamed of impacting the world and changing lives one at a time. I've stayed a student of personal growth and development. Why? Because I believe it has the power to change us individually, connect communities, be a catalyst to corporations, and transform countries around the world.

My passion in life is growing and equipping others to do remarkable things and lead significant and fulfilled lives. There's no greater mission for me. There's no greater mission for me. There's no higher goal than to help others realize their significance and potential.

But the key to unlocking that potential lies in your growth. You see, a better you is an unstoppable change agent—a transformed you creates a transformed world.

I'm all about transformation. That's why my team and I are committed to providing you the content and resources you need to become your better self. We are all-in on helping you make the right changes that change everything.

SCAN THE QR CODE
TO LEARN MORE

Learn more at
johnmaxwell.com

Maxwell Leadership corporate leadership development programs

Leadership shouldn't be a solo mission.
Great leaders work among their people, not above their people. We can help you build a team of strong leaders around you, creating better performance for the whole organization. Our proven process, based on John C. Maxwell's foundational leadership development principles, will help you fuel a leadership culture by aligning your organization around three essential elements:

Shared Leadership Principles
Shared Leadership Language
Shared Leadership Behaviors

The Maxwell Leadership® process
Our proprietary methodology is based on John C. Maxwell's The Five Levels of Leadership. It offers you and your team a comprehensive executive coaching and leadership development process that will inspire everyone to lead beyond their titles, find and develop other emerging leaders, and create a culture of leadership that propels your organization even when you're not in the room.

SCAN THE CODE TO LEARN MORE

Together, we work with you and your team to:

Listen
First, we listen and understand the unique challenges your team or organization is facing so we can develop the best solution for your needs.

Plan
We provide a detailed plan, customized to your business needs. In-depth assessments allow us to offer a carefully designed approach to your organization's development.

Deliver
A seasoned team of coaches, facilitators, and leadership specialists strive to exceed your expectations as they execute and deliver on the plan.

Impact
Unless our solutions are driving results in your business, we do not consider the work a success. Our commitment is not only to deliver, but to continue to evaluate our effectiveness by your organizational growth.

Learn more at
maxwellleadership.com